MW01232755

Country Boy
Conveniently
Wild

MARK LITTELL

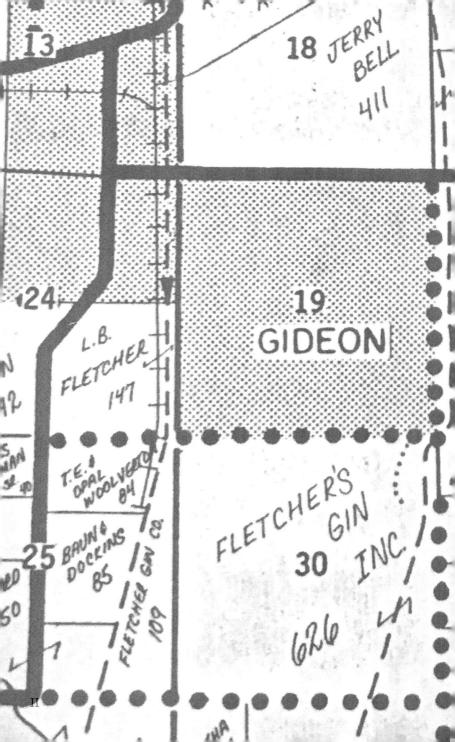

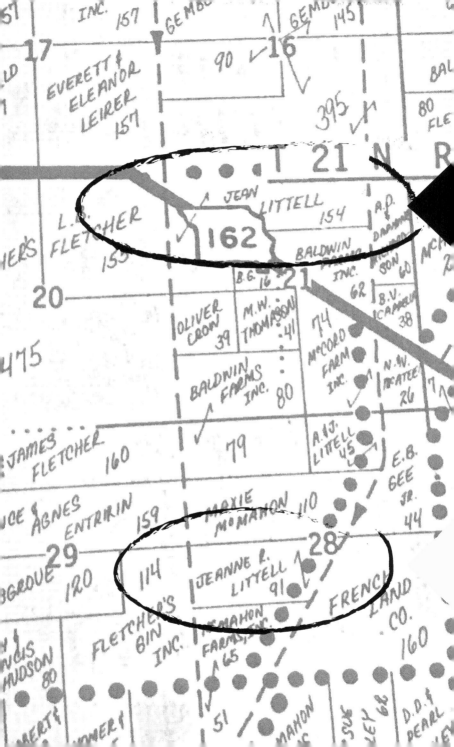

❝❝ After reading *Country Boy*, I felt as though I had relived my days growing up in the 'Bootheel'!!! Mr. Littell has done an incredible job telling the story of how life was growing up in swamp-east Missouri and explaining all of the "Bootheelism" ways. The era in which Country Boy was raised was possibly one of the best times ever. We learned respect and hard work, which obviously Mr. Littell is all about in his life and accomplishments.

-Jason Bean
5th Generation Farmer from the "Bootheel"

66 The Bootheel is a unique area of Missouri. It has characteristics of the south and the mid-west which makes this a one-of-a-kind place in many ways. This was a drained swamp in the upper Mississippi delta. Anyone interested in wanting to understand the economy and impact of these lower counties should read this book. This is a down home story told through the eyes of a Missourian who grew up in the Bootheel as only they can understand it. Mark has not forgotten his roots. You can hear his voice and twang come to life as he walks you through the Bootheel in the only way somebody would know who grew up here and lived it.

~ Senator Kit Bond
former Missouri Senator

66 Mark is an amazing person—former major league pitcher, entrepreneur and a brilliant guy. Most of all, I love how much he cares for and enjoys the people in his life, which he expresses with his own one-of-a-kind humor.

~ Barry LaBov
Founder, CEO of LaBov & Beyond Advertising,
Marketing and Training

If you purchase this book without a cover you should be aware that this book may have been stolen property and reported as "unsold and destroyed" to the publisher. In such case neither the author nor the publisher has received any payment for this "stripped book."

Copyright © 2018 by Mark Littell

All rights reserved. Except as permitted under the U.S. Copyright Act of 1976, no part of this publication may be reproduced, distributed, or transmitted in any form or by any means or stored in a database or retrieval system, without the prior written permission of the publisher.

Any registered trademarks referenced in this book are the property of their respective owners.

Illustrated by: Jacki Kellum
Edited by: kellie Coppolla
Book design by: Chellie Buzzeo
Published by: Bootheel Best, LLC

ISBN-13: 978-1981249657
ISBN-10: 981249656

Printed in the United States of America

First Edition: 2018

BOOTHEEL
MUD

Acknowledgements

Yes, this is my second try at this book thing but you gotta give credit to those that make the pieces of paper turn over and flip to that next page. Once again, thanks to the many folks that kept reading my broken-up and run-on sentences and made mention, "You might need some editing done"... you think?

I feel very fortunate to have Jerry Caulder write the Foreward. Jerry can double down as a former cultured "Redneck" but he had one of those chromosomes skip like a rock off water and he became a genius. Also, former Governor and Senator Kit Bond from the great state of Missouri, has a unique way of capturing and leading the many personalities from across the state. He seemed to like my down home sayings in the first read so I know he can talk 'Redneck'. Barry Labov was once a real live rock star and found out some other rock star guys had longer hair than he did so he just jingled along building a successful motivational company. Mark Farmer was sometimes out on the Gila River Indian Reservation growing cotton in Arizona and always talkin about ... "Where's the water?" Jason Bean is also a farmer that plants beans, lots of beans, down in Swamp East Missouri. Kinda funny that you've got a Farmer (Mark) and a Bean (Jason) tryin to keep their rows straight. Craig Coppola is still along and keeps pushin me on. He's also got another book under his belt.

Enter Kellie Coppola. Yes, this book is somewhat different than the first. In the first book, Kellie had to deal with all this baseball lingo and the names alone were tongue twisters from left field. In this reading, instead of going to a cultured country boy, we go backwards to me growing up in a half-done redneck mode. Yes, she carried my voice and kept it readable. I think she even got sick when going through one of my recipes but she smiled and laughed on most that ended with a real big bang.

The cover of both books to me makes a strong statement about the read. The first book I would have bought on the cover alone. This book has a much different storyline, and the layout and formatting are a touch different. Chellie Buzzeo brought some things into the look. And, she made me feel right at home with the barnwood, cotton, and soybeans. Imagination and creativity can be dangerous but also inquisitive. The search was on and kudos to you, Chellie.

There was this girl I went to school with in good ole Gideon. This was during the time of the Beatles, Elvis, and Tiny Tim. Yes, Jacki Kellum could tip-toe through the tulips with the best of 'em. She hitched a ride down to University of Mississippi, and spent some extra time drawin' all kinds a shit and walkin' away with a Masters in Art. The artwork that is sprinkled throughout the pages makes those chapters breathe. Not bad for a silly ass white girl that probably played the flute neck-ed out in some field.

Lyle Randolph is a bona fide redneck from Gideon that knows all the good fishin' spots and he's not too bad at trackin' down some old photos. When he's not being an amateur historian of the Bootheel he is the VP and manager of the Isle Casino in Cape Girardeau, MO. He just might step out back and throw a line in that big Mississippi River. Big river = big catfish.

Brother Eric was always in the mix. That mostly meant me getting us into trouble. He would either follow or I would drag him along on these escapades just so I wouldn't be the lone dumbass when things didn't fall right. Yes, Brother Eric is still breathing and lives in Memphis and still has definite redneck tendencies and flashbacks.

I feel very fortunate to have Jerry Caulder write the Foreword. Jerry can double down as a former cultured redneck, but he had one of those chromosomes skip like a rock off water and he became a genius. Barry Labov was once a rock star and found out some other rock star guys had longer hair than he did so he just jingled along building a well-motivated company. Mark Farmer was sometimes out on the Gila River Indian Reservation planting cotton in Arizona and always talkin' about,

"Where's the water?" Craig Coppola is still along and pushin' me on.

Over the fall, I drove Sanna down to the Bootheel for the first time. This city girl was taking a gander at all this flat farmland while soakin' up the cotton that was still covered and stacked in the fields. All of a sudden, she pointed and asked me, "What's that big red piece of machinery?" That, my dear, is what we call a fucking cotton picker. She did say I was getting better at the English language, but held her ground on me being crass. I knew what it meant this time.

Roscoe, my German Shorthair and trusted companion, is still at my side when I'm peckin' away. His vocabulary has improved from 200 words to an additional 25. If I have a misfire with this writing thing, he muzzles my elbow. He looks up at me with those soft brown eyes that speak volumes, "There's a better way." Yep, this dog can still hunt.

Foreword

It's often said that you can take the boy out of the country, but you can't take the country out of the boy. More often as not, when someone says that it's not meant to be a compliment. It might occasionally mean "salt of the earth," but more often than that it'll mean "unsophisticated." That's okay. My father was unsophisticated. His diet was literally farm to table, but there aren't too many people who consider themselves "foodies" who would have appreciated our diet enough to include it on their instagram accounts except out of irony. My son relishes telling his friends in the very sophisticated city of Los Angeles about the time we were stuck in Gideon during a snowstorm over Thanksgiving and ate squirrel and dumplings. My son, you see, is sophisticated. He grew up in San Diego, but since San Diego wasn't big enough, he moved to Los Angeles. His sons are very sophisticated, they started eating sushi when they were five and think it's hilarious that I think sushi is disgusting.

I don't know whether my father would have eaten sushi or not, though, let's face it, probably not. But he wouldn't have cared a bit if someone else ate it and enjoyed it. It was none of his business. He liked bologna on white bread, not that he cared what you thought about that. He started every day with a cup of coffee.

He didn't drink it from the cup, he drank it from the saucer. He'd pour the coffee into the saucer, and lift it to his mouth without spilling a drop. I thought that's how people were supposed to drink coffee. Only later did I learn that he drank it like that because with more surface area it cooled faster and he was able to drink it sooner and get to work.

Now I ask you, is that unsophisticated, or is that science?

Much to the astonishment of the people who knew me well as a boy, I've somehow made it to seventy-five years old. The vast majority of those years have been spent outside of the small town where both Mark Littell, the accomplished author of this book, and I grew up, Gideon, Missouri. In fact I've lived almost half of them in San Diego, California, which is about as far away from Gideon as you can get, in terms of lifestyle. But in all those years away from Gideon, that small town and the lessons I learned there, have never left me.

What brought me to San Diego was the opportunity to run a biotech company named Mycogen. How did I, the dirt poor son of a Missouri sharecropper, end up running a biotech company? How did Mark become a professional athlete, entrepreneur, and designer of an athletic cup that can take a 90mph baseball? Yeah, think about that for a second. The answer, I think, starts with my dad's morning saucer of coffee.

Growing up with a lot of work and few, if any, luxuries, means that you have to work smart. You have neither time, nor energy to waste. Picking watermelons and putting them in a truck, carefully, during the hottest month of the year is not a fun job. By necessity and design you don't get shade in a field. You bend over and lift a heavy watermelon again and again. If you were to do this, walk to the truck, climb in the truck, stack the melon, and go back to do it all over time and again, you'd either die or just want to.

So, you set up a line, pass the melons down, hand them up to a guy in the truck who stacks them, and work it this way, changing positions in the line every so often so nobody gets stuck with the worst positions for a full day.

You also don't complain. Nothing slows down time and makes a watermelon heavier than listening to someone complain. You are a part of a team. Everyone has their own job to do, and everyone does every job at some point. There's no point in complaining. You have to pick all the watermelons, and when they're picked, you're finished. So you work cooperatively, and if anyone has a good idea about how make the job faster or easier, you listen. This is what "you can't take the country out of the boy," means to me. It's not about a type of music you like, or the type of clothes you wear. It's your attitude towards sacrifice and accomplishments.

It's the choice you make when you hear a good idea. Gideon taught me that it doesn't matter who thought of a good idea, it's the thinking and the idea that counts. When someone says, "Hey, here's how we can make these watermelons lighter," you don't immediately start looking for ways the idea won't work, and you don't become resentful that someone else thought of it first. You're just happy that the watermelons might get lighter. And if it's not a perfect idea, you work together to refine it.

Mark Littell didn't write this book to glorify himself or his accomplishments. He wrote it to help us refine ourselves. He knows what it takes to get that little bit extra on his fastball, and how that will help not just himself, but his whole team. And he knows that by helping his team, he's also helping himself. It's country science.

I know you'll enjoy reading this as I have. Mark is not just a great writer, he's country smart. And in my experience, that's my favorite kind of smart. It's the kind of smart that keeps you from burning your tongue on boiling hot coffee, and makes a thousand watermelons lighter. It's what we need more of right now.

~Dr. Jerry Caulder
Father of Agricultural Bio Technology

Our Connection:
Jerry Caulder and Mark Littell

You will find out that we had plenty of space to spread our wings. I grew up on No. 7 Ditch and Mark grew up on No. 5 Ditch. As the crow flies we were about four miles apart. My expertise would be in science, cotton and soybeans, and the weed business. Mark on the other hand would end up throwing a baseball and down the line his creative side would blossom in many different ways.

One thing Mark and I experienced was that we had the same bus driver even though I had a few years on him. Carlee Moore, the bus driver, was top notch. He kept everybody in line either coming or going. Mark told me about the time when he was getting on the bus with a tall slender can with a screen on top. Carlee asked Mark, "What you got in there?"

"Something for science class, Mr. Moore."

Well Mark didn't get real specific, so he ended up carrying on a big fat three-foot water moccasin. Word had gotten out that Mark had a real deal of a tester walking the halls of Gideon elementary. He, along with a following of knowingly curious boys, reached his fifth grade homeroom. Mrs. Shock was standing at the door way and said, "What you got there?" Without saying a word he just popped the top and threw out that big black muddy moccasin in the back of the classroom. Yeah, you might say, "Shit hit the fan" and of course all the girls just hit the wall. He said Mrs. Shock's face was looking like a potential stroke victim. Thank you Mr. Moore for not asking what was in that can.

Carlee was good with me as well. In the fall when the ducks were flying I would duck hunt just about anywhere. To save time, I would step onto the bus and Carlee would say, "Jerry, that shotgun's not loaded is it?" I would answer, "No Carlee, it's not and I got the shells in my pocket." "Alright! Give me the shotgun." He'd stand it up between him and the pull for the STOP sign. After school I'd take the ride but he'd drop me off on the Floodways. He gave me my shotgun back and I'd generally knock down a couple if not more of any kind of duck. Back then we were meat hunters; want to eat, you better shoot it. Carlee would swing back by the house after his run and check in to see if I had scored. Sometimes he might help me clean 'em and I'd pass a couple his way.

You'll find out that this was a tough area with good people but we survived and even cleaned up well when needed. Farmers, ranchers, and even city slickers are definitely going to like what's in this fun book. Yep, they're all good folks down this way, maybe some of that Bootheel mud will stick to the glowing side of your life.

Introduction

One thing about dynamite: it doesn't just go "boom"—it can *roar*. A loud, angry noise that's meaner than any cat in the jungle. The ground we were standing on *rattled,* shaking every inch of me like I was on a carnival ride. Then the fireworks started.

You could almost feel every stick go off. One, two, three, four…all the way up to eighteen sticks of fiery dynamite. This was a head-jerkin' moment watchin' all these chunks flyin' every direction. It was all very exciting for about five seconds, just like a movie. But then it was back to reality. And the reality was that Eric and I *weren't quite far enough* from ground zero. Little pieces of splintery wood and dirt were flying into our space and soon we were both covered with fine, granular bits of dirt, with some remains of fragmented oak wood stuck on our t-shirts.

As the debris settled, and the roar of the explosion faded into a nasty sizzling sound, I turned to Eric with wide eyes.

Holy shit.

XX

Weeds, Beans, and Cotton

When you get a third of the way through this book, you're going to think, "I haven't seen or read anything on baseball." It's true that I played baseball most of my life, but growing up on a farm, my hands and feet were first used to dig into the earth. Weeds had to be pulled, cotton had to be chopped (thinned out), and soybeans had to be cultivated and nurtured. And that's what this book is about. Those early, formative years that turned me into the Country Boy who eventually made it to the Big Leagues.

The formation of a person's character, for the most part, occurs at an early age, and it takes a collection of interesting folks floating through to help seal your fate and mindset. Growing up in the Bootheel would give me some of those mainstays required to journey through this short life on earth.

My brother Eric and I seemed to have a corner on being at the right place at the right time when we were growing up. We got into a lot of peculiar places and situations, with trouble usually in the mix because we always had to take that extra step to get to the real adventure. We got around and opened our eyes and minds to anything moving or not moving. We were explorers.

Yup, we were curious, mischievous, and just down right ornery sometimes. I'm sure I'll have some animal rights activist camped at my front door after this book comes out. Aw, well. Read on and take a ride through some of the best farmland in the world, and follow the adventures of a Country Boy: Conveniently Wild.

Dad, mom, me and Blaylock

Bootheel playground.

Gideon Anderson International Harvester FOR SALE left to right - Wheat drills, International Pick-up, and two combines.

Me and Eric

AUCTIONEER
FOR ALL TYPE SALES
ALAN LITTELL
TALLAPOOSA, MO.
Phone 2501, Risco, Mo.
Reasonable Rates

The Lineup

Most barbers who cut my hair will say, "Do you know you have a 'cow lick' on the back of your head? Kinda hard to keep down, huh?"

Yeah, I've heard that one before. But just because I have a cow lick doesn't mean I was born in a barn and a cow licked me on the head when I came outta the chute! I was born in Cape Girardeau, Missouri in a hospital. The doctor who dragged me out meant to slap me on the ass to get me screamin' but probably missed and hit me in the head. That's how I got the cow lick and some really weird ideas about the light of the world to come.

When you're on the top end of the Mississippi Delta, you are still Southern to the bone. We didn't have it all but we had a farm and things got better as the years moved by. Yes sir, you always counted your blessings.

Growing up, the actors in my life consisted of my dad, my mom, my brother Eric, and several other colorful characters from the town of Gideon, Missouri and surrounding area. My father Alan grew up in the "Bootheel" and was a farmer who fought in the Korean War. To sum up Dad, he was God, country, and take care of your family. The Korean War was not so forgiving, and he got shot up bad. He rarely ever talked about the War, but the brace he wore on his hand and forearm was a constant reminder of what he'd been through.

The official report of Dad's service as a Marine came to me years later from the chaplain at Arlington. Dad's platoon was under attack from enemy fire in a cemetery. They had been there a while and realized that they needed to retreat, but were under heavy fire. Dad stayed behind, acting as a decoy as the others fled. While lying behind a headstone, he waved his right hand briefly to attract attention while the others left. At some point his wrist was hit by enemy fire. He too fled the cemetery, but was also hit by shrapnel and went down in "no man's land."

Our marines thought my father had bought it, but they embraced "No Man Left Behind." An American Indian and a black man dragged my dad out of this so-called dead zone and ultimately pulled him back to safety, guaranteeing that he would make it back to the farm. When Dad went down, Mom was three months pregnant with me in tow. After I came out screamin', Brother Eric would follow a year and sixteen days later. Thank you, God.

Mom was good for Dad—she held on hard and prayed when he woke up yelling in the middle of the night. As time passed, this part of the ordeal got better but he did suffer.

Both Mom and Dad started school together in the first grade and both probably gave each other a lot shit over the next twelve years in the good ole Gideon School District. Out of high school, my mom attended college at Illinois Wesleyan University for one year where she majored in music. Then, out of the clear blue, she decided a change was necessary, and she switched over to the field of nursing. Mom could still play the piano and flute well, and she was succinct in striking the keys firmly. Eric and I used to hope the damn piano would take a beating so she wouldn't start banging on us. She went to St. Louis and enrolled in the nursing program at Deaconess Hospital. She passed the boards and came out throwin' needles. Both Eric and I also tried not to cough around Mom because we knew we could have easily become a moving dartboard.

Mom and Dad both played sports. Mom ran track, and she could outrun me until my thirteenth birthday. I had my growth spurts and did get faster, but it was a banged-up knee from a fender bender that got me over the hump, so she lost a step on that one. But Mom was tough. Dad played baseball and basketball. He was awarded the Purple Heart, Bronze Star, and Presidential citation. Today, both Mom and Dad are buried in Arlington National Cemetery.

When we resided outside Wardell, we lived in a small house on a farm that we leased. When you stepped out on either the front or back porch all you would see was green fields of soybeans as far as you could see. We spent six years in this area. With Dad as a sharecropper (leasing the land) and Mom a registered nurse, we were stacked up with most of the folks just trying to figure it out and get ahead. There was no glitz or glamour. But for my brother and I it didn't seem that way. For us, everything was top-notch. There was family support not too far away, and we had a lot of love.

Most folks in this area had it real tough, and many lived below the poverty line. The whole Bootheel ran high with poverty, which never went unnoticed. You could see the cluttered-up front yards, the run-down vehicles, and kids that had a little less food than most.

Then there were borderline folks who were trying to do the best with what they had been dealt.

By the time I started first grade the area started to show growth. Business was steady and slowly the scale would move toward the middle. I even remember when we got our first television. Dad had to put up a pole next to the house to get the antenna high enough to reach the airwaves. If you really wanted to tune into a certain network, Dad would go outside and turn the pole some until Mom hollered, "You got it." The rabbit ears that came with this contraption were just useless. At the time we got two channels, then a couple of years later we could tune into three networks. Yes sir, we were livin' in high cotton.

One station in particular that we watched closely was the CBS Evening News with Walter Cronkite, who was often called the most trusted man in America. At the end of the telecast, his sign off would settle us in for the night. It was true and it was simple—"And that's the way it is." Walter Cronkite's voice gave us a safe feeling for many years. He was born in Missouri so I figured he must have been a good guy.

Let's bring Brother Eric into play. Eric was a catcher and he caught me in Little League, high school, and American Legion baseball. He also caught at Mississippi State and was drafted twice, though he chose not to sign. I called him to see if he was going to sign when he got drafted low in the June Major League Draft. He paused and said, "Let me tell you something, that's a bunch of shit what you do." He ended up choosing the right path.

Eric, for the most part, was my best buddy and usually got the short end of the stick from my side. Starting in our early years when mistakes were made, shit came rolling downhill, earning us the nickname, "The Gruesome Twosome."

One of the hardest things for me to overcome and deal with was the fact that I had ADD (Attention Deficit Disorder). Of course, they knew nothing about ADD in the fifties, sixties, seventies, and most of the eighties. At some point, someone started to figure out why a few kids and adults had a hard time focusing on a task, and acted like an overall pain in the ass. I found out at age 46 that I was leader of the pack. When put on the right meds, I immediately saw the world for the first time. Twenty minutes after this pill went down the hatch and settled, everything opened up and I realized I'd missed out on a lot. I went from barely reading to cannot read enough. I look at it this way: I've got 46 years of making up to do.

Farm life in mid-America during my upbringing was a blast in more ways than one, as you will find out. My life in particular was about bravery, courage, and only a little common sense (very little). These people who came into my life helped me step across the line. They pushed me, whether on the field or off. I had countless sounding boards, and it was fantastic.

The Lineup

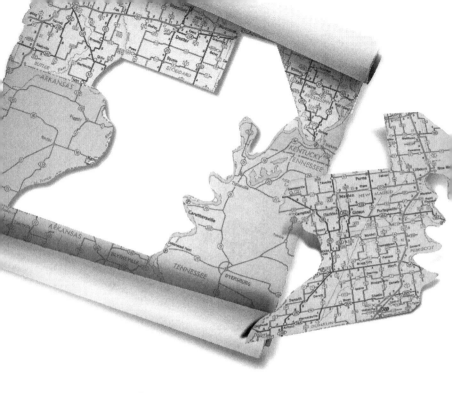

Getting a Lay
of the Land

To the locals who live in the flats of Southeast Missouri, the area where I grew up was called the "Bootheel." It's the part that hangs down into Arkansas, or as we like to say, "It's the part Arkansas didn't want." There are seven counties that make up this massive area that hugs the Mississippi River. It also produces over 50% of Missouri's entire crop load, including soybeans and cotton.

Our one-stoplight town of Gideon had a population of around a thousand. A few passing motorists might slow down to gawk, and some would say that it was "a wide spot in the road" but that small-town environment was unlimited in so many ways.

This was once swampland, and the DNA that runs through these folks' veins is a little different. If you happen to spot a local walkin' around barefoot, go ahead, look down and take a gander at their feet—it's just possible they got some webbing between those toes formed over generations of trekkin' through mud, water, and silt. Yeah, we can scoot across that swamp ground real well.

We lived just off No. 5 Ditch, three miles east of Gideon. We were pretty much in the center of these seven counties that made up an area called the "Little River Drainage District," second only to the Egyptian Nile in size. The lines for the Bootheel's massive piece of real estate were drawn from Crowley Ridge just eleven miles south of Cape Girardeau as the northern border. The Arkansas line held the southern border, the Mississippi River held it in on the east, and the St. Francis River detained it to the west. Most consider the three lower counties—Pemiscot, Dunklin, and New Madrid—to be the real "Bootheel" and the folks there are generally pleasant but can be a real kickass type when riled up.

Story has it, there was this Indian chief named Reelfoot that hung out just across the river in Tennessee. They say he got bent out of shape about somethin' (probably some chick), and stomped his foot. He must've got his message across, because they say his stomp is what started the New Madrid Quake of 1811.

This quake lasted off-and-on for almost three months before it finally started dyin' down in February of 1812. It jumbled up the land mass, and formed Reelfoot Lake in Tennessee (so the story must be true). It even turned the Mississippi River backwards at one point, and rang church bells as far away as Connecticut. This is what formed that huge basin known as the Missouri Bootheel, which would become some of the best farmland in the country.

The center of the quake, the "New Madrid Fault Line," is a dandy. Even to this day it'll give out two or three noticeable tremors a year. Yep, and it's larger than the San Andreas fault—California beach boys got nothin' on us Bootheel rednecks. New Madrid (by the way, we say "New Mad-rid" while outsiders say "New Ma-drid"—those folks seem to think they're cultured) was named after the capital of Spain by Desoto when he came up the Mississippi. There must've been a pretty good Indian skirmish up here, because there's a mound right outside of New Madrid with Indians as well as conquistadors buried inside. The University of

Missouri came down and scanned the mound and did an excavation to reveal all the goodies.

But anyway, the "Boot" as we locals call it, was pretty much an uninhabitable swamp after the quake. Anything and everything grew untouched for the next hundred years: oak, hickory, gum, a few walnut trees, and of course, when you have a swamp you also have cypress. If we had a cypress tree on any of our farmland in Gideon (west of New Madrid), it stayed. It basically signified that it was good ground, and they were pretty to the eye as well.

By the early 1900's, there were a few large lumber companies that came in and took what was there for the taking, and pieces of land were bought up for the lumber. There were a few folks up around Cape Girardeau who wanted to see if they could clear this swampland and turn it into some kind of productive farming.

As an end result, the owners in these seven counties eventually paid a tax levy that would go to clearing and creating diversion channels. In 1914, they started the cleanup and dredging of over 1,000 miles of ditches with 300 miles of levees to hold the water back. It was finished in 1928. The project was larger, with more dirt being moved, than the dredging and building of the Panama Canal. We say "timing is everything"—a big "You bet!" to that. The Panama Canal was completed in late October of 1913, and you might have thought all those massive digging and dirt-moving machines would have just sat idle in Panama, rustin' away. But there was no rest for these machines, and many of the people who finished the Canal came north to do what would end up being a bigger project: the Bootheel of Missouri. To make the Mississippi levee hold back all this water was quite a chore. They came in with the big draglines and dirt movers and stayed after it from sunrise to sunset.

Yep, you drive through the Boot today you'll still see areas of swampland and thickets. While some of those places held standing, murky water, the high ground, on the other hand, was generally damp, with all kinds of wildlife, yet still serene and quiet. If you sat down and stayed still, the swamp would gravitate to a calmness—I found peace in these most peculiar surroundings. Around dusk you could sit down and listen to crickets chirpin', cicadas buzzin', and the bull frogs croakin' over on No.5 ditch. Plus those damn mosquitos. The water of the Mississippi River had its own issues, yet those first few ditches that moved the water out made for some good gardens early on. As more swamp was cleared and this network of ditches was put in place, row crops followed. Then one day, finally, "They had a garden party."

The Bootheel is floating on one big underground stream. Water is abundant—throw down a point well 12-14 feet and you got drinkin' water. Occasionally, brother Eric and I would drop one in the ground for a pump near a house or somebody's garden. The starter pipe was two and a half inches in diameter and five feet long, with a point that had holes and a filter. Get it straight and bang it down a couple of feet. Next, we'd go to the high road and stand on top of the big back tire of a tractor and just start adding five-foot sections and keep banging away with this homemade ram that weighed around 25 pounds. It took a lot of pounding to get down to the water table and this is where trading off was good because it would definitely wear your ass out. Once we got down to the water table, we put a Briggs and Stratton 3HP engine on top of that last pipe, pull the cord and crank 'er up. Now we got panther piss. (There's a figure of speech you probably don't hear too often—if you don't know it, panther piss heals and cures anything.)

Anyhow, the water shot out of that pipe fast, in a stream of rusty-brown iced tea. It took about two minutes to clear up, but then the water was great—it even came with iron, soybean herbicides, insecticides, cotton defoliant, engine oil from equipment, and maybe some antifreeze—like I said, great. Yep, this tea concoction could change your brain waves. By the time you hit age 50, you might start talking like Pee Wee Herman. Or maybe you'll just discover that you did a full circle, and that you now have the brain of a five-year-old. Needless to say, the EPA ain't got nothin' goin' on with the Bootheel farmer.

Sterling Price Reynolds was one of the founding supervisors and lead engineers who put in years of labor to make the Little River Drainage District function. He helped build and maintain these mounds of dirt, holding back the big waters when the rains came and threatened to flood the Bootheel. From the headwaters in Cape Girardeau, he built that mound and took it down past the Arkansas line. When I was a child, Mr. Reynolds became a patient in the Haiti Memorial Hospital. Since our mother was an RN and worked at the hospital, she told us about Mr. Reynolds' background and the role he played in developing the drainage district. Mom said he had many stories of building and being on that levee from dusk to dawn, and for him it was a labor of love. It must have been in his blood, because he started the project when he was in his mid-fifties.

Both Eric and I went down to the hospital to meet Mr. Reynolds—Mom wanted us to meet him, but said if he was asleep we shouldn't wake him. We walked into the room, and he was under this oxygen tent (at that time, they didn't have the oxygen tubes that wrapped around your ears and stuck in your nose). Smoking was a definite no-no in this room. Light up a cig and it would incinerate anybody or anything in the room ... nobody was interested in getting a free cremation.

We walked up and saw that he was out of it (hell, he should have been out of it—he was born in 1862). We backed out quietly, and had to be satisfied with just the stories that Mom would keep passing along. A year later, Mom came home a little sad. Mr. Reynolds had just passed away. I have to say, it sure sounded like he led a great life. He died in 1968, at 106 years old, with a hell of a lot of accomplishments. Mom asked him, "What's your secret to longevity Mr. Reynolds?" He said, "Well Ms. Jeanne, I figure it's me getting up every mornin' and walkin' those levees from sun-up to sundown."

There were over 1,000 miles of ditches and 300 levees built to make this whole thing work, and the Army corps of Engineers has kept it clean since 1931. All these pathways and fingers of smaller ditches were capable of moving water in sizable proportions, but when a couple inches of rain landed in the Bootheel, the ditches would swell to almost half-full; four inches would get some flooding and bring the muddy water toward the top, but a six-inch downpour had disaster written all over it. It meant that the Mighty Mississippi was getting so backed-up with these massive amounts of fast-running water with nowhere to go, that it just overflowed and kicked the water back up into the lower seven counties.

But when they stopped the flooding and got rid of the standing water, they built a baseball field. In the center of the field was a mound. And one day, a few years later, I found it.

Eric, me and Fritz

Trouble for the Gruesome Twosome

First, let me say this about Eric; he had a problem with his throat as a little guy. There was a growth on his throat that the doctors would remove when the time was right. We're not sure what was going on or exactly when it needed to be removed, so he talked funny until he was around five years old. It was kinda like Daffy Duck, and the only person who could really understand what he was saying was me. When he got excited, you would have to bear down to really focus and try to read between the lines to figure out what was coming out of that little pie hole. Sometimes it was like he was talking Egyptian.

A most dramatic incident would happen on a very hot Saturday afternoon when living on the Wardell farm. The year was 1958 and dad had made a run up to Gideon. We didn't have air conditioning so it was extra hot unless you were right in front of a window fan. Being around our first dog, Duke, made the day go fast and the playtime worthwhile. We found shade in the back porch, and just when you'd think everything was calm on the home front, all hell would break loose.

Mom was inside talking on the phone in the front bedroom, which had one large window facing the front yard. She was talking to Grandma Reiffer and I was sitting on the edge of the bed listening in, curious as always. The first phone line we had was on a party line. It was a whole lot cheaper—no doubt about it, a private line was for the big dogs. On a party line there might be six people linked together all with access to this one line. If they were slippery and smooth about picking up the receiver, they could eavesdrop. They would listen in on your conversation or quite possibly just join in to stay up with the gossip. If someone had an emergency, you would just tell 'em to get off. Somebody usually started screamin', something like, "Hey moron, we got a real problem on this end, clear the line, gotta call the hospital."

On this very hot afternoon we had all the floor fans going. Mom and Grandma Reiffer were talking about anything that moved—country folk could gossip up a storm once they warmed up to you. You'd hear all kinds of bullshit and eventually walk away thinking these people were so deranged maybe they should be in a movie.

All of a sudden, Mom and I saw Eric fly by the front window, but we thought nothing of it except he was basically off limits to the front of the house. A minute later, we saw him pass in front of the window again as he continued to haul ass. Another minute passed and for the third time we watched him go by the window. Finally he was starting to slow down. He had gone past the porch because we had a window on the side of the house, and I was now tracking him while Mom was still on the phone.

Finally, he stopped, came back to the front door and walked in to where Mom was on the phone. His face was red and sweating, and he was just panting like a dog. His hands were clasped and then they went to flailing. With this growth in his throat he was moving like I had never seen him before. All kinds of mumbo-jumbo started coming out of that more than exaggerated orifice.

Mom said, "Eric, slow down, Eric, slow down, Eric, sweetheart, please slow down."

He must have been speaking in tongues because Mom couldn't figure out hide nor hair of what the hell he was saying. Finally, she called in the interpreter. "Mark, what is your brother saying?"

"Eric, say it one more time," I yelled at him.

He had a lot of gibberish comin' out of that opening but eventually I got it. I said to Mom, "Eric says there's a big black water moccasin out under the swing."

He later told me that he was hanging upside down and it was moving toward him. Hell, the little shit fell down to the ground and luckily missed landing on the snake. In all the hoopla, Eric couldn't think straight so he started running around the house, kinda like Forrest Gump. He finally tuckered out after he missed the front door three times.

Mom got into one of her hysterical moods and suddenly she was scrambling to get us into the '51 Ford. She headed to our farmhand Able's house which was 200 yards down the road from us. Able saw us drive up and made it out to the front porch. "Hi Ms. Jeanne," he said, but Mom didn't have time to say hi, she was too bent out of shape and talking like Eric. Able told Mom to slow down, but I was not asked to interpret.

Mom finally spit it out, and he went back inside the house to grab his single shot .22 savage rifle. He jumped into the front seat as we went back to the house for the big hunt. We all got out of the car and headed to the last known location of this guy. But the snake wasn't near the swing. We walked over to the wooden back steps, and Able said, "He probably moved toward the steps to get under the house to cool off and maybe head toward the hydrant with the water puddle around it. This sucker is on the move."

Able asked Mom for a hammer. "I'm going to pop that bottom step off. Go in through the front door to get the hammer, there's a gap in the steps. Don't want that rascal to bite ya on the foot."

Mom brought out the hammer and Able hooked the claw of the hammer under the middle of the bottom step, and jerked up. He didn't want to pry it off, too much time for the snake to be in that very aggressive attack mode.

I've heard some folks say that the water moccasin is a rather docile snake. Well my theory on that assertion is that they must not have seen these guys comin' at them, because they really get pissed off if you're in their area, and to top it all off, they'll stalk you. They're docile when they're dead. And, you definitely don't want one sinking his fangs into your hide. They are a never-ending strike machine and they just keep comin' back for more of you.

Able popped that board off of the lower step and you bet there was a beautiful, three-foot moccasin that was definitely pissed off, coiled, and ready to take us on. He showed his telltale pinkish white mouth when he opened it up. Some folks call them "cotton mouths."

Able said, "Keep your distance." He went at the snake with a shovel but it backed down fast and scurried under the house. "Ms. Jeanne, I'm goina pop the skirting off the side of the house and try to see if I can find him. He's probably heading for the water hydrant on the opposite side of the house, so back the boys off, maybe I can get a shot off."

He popped the skirting and got down on his knees with the .22 and started lookin'. "There he is," Able called. "Right where I thought he would be." You could see under the house because there was a gap between the skirting and the ground; sunlight would come through so you could see a silhouette of anything especially if it moved. Able set his sight on the target, pulled the trigger and we were now minus one fat water moccasin.

Able got that moccasin and Mom was calm for the moment but living in a small community and growing up on a farm had moments of excitement. You had to love it.

A year and a half later, Eric had his growth removed but he still talked like he had marbles in his mouth. He had to see a speech pathologist until he was in the ninth grade. Matter of fact, both of us had to see the speech pathologist because I had lost the hearing in my right ear when I was twelve. I picked up some kinda strange bacteria swimming in our pond. The state made us drain it after that. After spending ten days in the hospital, the doctors suggested that I go to Central Institute of the Deaf in St. Louis for six weeks when I was thirteen. I went just in case the other ear would go.

In the end, Eric couldn't talk and I couldn't hear. Whenever I went onto a major league baseball field, I never heard what the fans would say, and when I'm in a crowd I can't hear shit. I would just smile and keep moving when I was near the stands. I'm sure some of 'em said, "Littell, you suck" or "Littell, you're an asshole." Normal stuff at a big league park. I know that I probably pissed off a few folks with my good-natured humor. I give credit to the "Man Upstairs" for that one.

Trouble for the Gruesome Twosome

Rampaging Cow

Mama Sally was our grandmother, Dad's mom, and both Eric and I always liked going up to see her. It was new territory to explore and about ten miles north from our house. Dad ran her farm and kept everything in order on this 160-acre piece of real estate. It was the same as anywhere else in the Bootheel in that it had terrific soil, but Mama Sally also had some big trees and a huge barn to run around in, and Eric and I found this very appealing.

We were twelve and thirteen and ripe for getting into trouble. It was one of those days, kinda sultry and overcast. We were moving a little slow and hoped we would get some action. We were looking for something dangerous but it just wasn't in the cards for the moment. We went over to the big barn and foraged around in it, then maneuvered through the old hay bales bored stiff from not finding a snake or a coon. We scuttled butt-down the inside of the barn where all we found were dried up cow turds. We finally made it around to the other sheds. We were always trying to find mischief and it was on a crawl today until Dad hollered, "Boys, get over here."

Now we perked up real quick.

"You see that cow?" he said when we got to him. "That's Mrs. Pettigrew's milk cow. Throw a rope around it and get it back into her barn. And while you two are over there, fix the fence where she's getting out."

Yeah baby, we finally got some action. Mrs. Pettigrew lived just across the gravel road from Mama Sally. Her husband had passed away so she had trouble keeping up with all the excitement that came with a farm. It's the little stuff that was overlooked. Running a farm is just a never-ending job. One thing about living in a farming community, though, is that people would generally help other people, and we did live in the Bible belt, so, help your neighbor.

Hardly anybody in the Bootheel has a milk cow, but this one was staring us in the face. She didn't run so getting the rope on her was easy. Eric and I waltzed her back to the barn and started looking for the problem. It turned out the gate latch needed to be tightened. We found tools in the barn and fixed the latch. Finished. When we went back to check on the cow we got this bright idea to have some fun with her.

My dad and uncles would set around the table and tell stories about putting turpentine on a dog's butt and watching him scoot across the yard. They called it "dog push." Turpentine can get hot if you put it in the right spot. So, I got the same idea to do it to the cow. We went back to the tool shed in the barn to look for turpentine—most farmers had all kinds of concoctions tucked away in the many different drawers, shelves, and nooks that were added to accumulate all this crap. Bingo! We found the turpentine.

Well, we got the ole corn cob doctored up and got the cow cornered. I lifted the tail and hit the mark as Eric wanted nothing to do with this dastardly deed. We backed off and nothing was happening. We looked at each other, a little disappointed.

Then, watch out! Hold on! Now we were seeing some movement, side to side. Then she got her butt on the ground as the ole girl pulled herself with the front hoofs and started scooting across the barn.

Whoa, now we were getting worried. At this point the heifer stood up and was acting up and kickin'. She was getting a little crazy so we exited fast. We ran over to Mama Sally's house for dinner (lunch), and washed our hands real good, trying to act innocent.

In walked Dad, and as he sat down he asked, "You guys got the cow back in the barn?"

"Yes sir, fixed the latch as well."

"That's good, I'll go over and check your work out after lunch."

Mama Sally said a lunch prayer, and Eric and I were thinking about her doing a few extra prayers for us. We both had a feelin' that the Almighty would need that extra push today. So far, so good, but we knew it wasn't going to last.

Mrs. Pettigrew showed up not long after and was outside yelling, "Alan, oh Alan, are you there?" through the screen door.

Dad said, "Come on in."

She made it through the screen door and said, "Alan, my cow's gone mad, she's tearing up the barn."

"I'll be right there, Mrs. Pettigrew." Dad walked around the corner and turned to look back at us. "What did you two do to the cow?"

"Turpentine and a corn cob," I said automatically. "Wanted to see if it worked. We heard you and Uncle Bill and Uncle Jack laughin' about it when you put it on dogs."

Mama Sally was just shakin' her head. I'm sure she had gone through this same scenario when my dad was young.

"I'll be back and deal with you two later. Stay in the house," Dad said.

Holy shit, we both knew the wrath of God was coming down on us. Dad got the cow calmed down and he told Mrs. Pettigrew that he'd take care of setting the boys straight.

She said, "Now Alan, you take it easy on those boys. They really didn't know any better and the cow quit givin' milk over a year ago." Way to go Mrs. Pettigrew, thanks for the vote to take it easy on us, but we knew very well all that sweet talk was up in smoke.

A few years later, I felt this could have fallen under the category of generational sin. We figured the cow's ass was sore but we most definitely got the worst end of the deal. Eric and I came to the conclusion that the cow shoulda been turned into hamburger anyway when it stopped givin' milk. This was our first and definitely last time dealing with the misbehavior of an animal.

REDNECK DISCLAIMER

Yes, I was a bad boy at age thirteen. All sorts of odd feelings combined with a rampant brain in tow pushed me over the edge. Do not place any blame on brother Eric for following my lead. He is a kind and gentle human being. I love animals and recognize I was at fault and this was more than a worthless and dastardly deed done in the name of having some fun. For all animal activists that will be protesting, please do not spend too much time on my lawn and take the signs with you when you leave.

Bet-Cha

*O*ur family was a product of rural America. This next section is devoted to one category of rural life or the good life: RECREATION. When one reveals the news, "I grew up on a farm," the next topic of conversation is, "What the hell did you do for fun?" Country folks can become very creative when it comes to recreation and I am not just talking about school, church, or family-organized events because the only organization to any of these events was that there was no organization.

Recreation in rural America, especially below the Mason-Dixon Line, began most of the time with one word: bet-cha. Most challenges were accepted by an opponent who came back with something like, "bet-cha I can" or "bet-cha you're wrong" or some form of a bet-cha acknowledgement.

There are two categories of recreation: (1) black and white and (2) I give. There are many different types of recreational challenges within each of these categories. The rules consisted of, well, there were no rules and most challenges ended in a clear-cut winner. It was black and white with no questions asked as this was the quickest form of recreational victory. The other type of challenge, I give, was a sort of participation until one couldn't go any longer. Literally, this recreation usually ended in cuts, scrapes, burns, bruises, broken bones, unconsciousness, or coughing up blood.

An example of the black and white recreation is, "I bet-cha that blackbird will fly left when I throw this rock." There are only two responses that are adequate in this bet-cha recreational call, and that boils down to a "call me out" throw down from the competitor—that is, "I don't give a crap"—or "I bet-cha the bird flies the other direction." If the reply from the competitor is, "I bet-cha the bird flies the other direction," then it's game on and let the contest begin...provided the blackbird hasn't flown away. The rock is thrown and it's black or white which way the bird flies, and we have a winner.

The "I don't give a crap" response ends the recreational challenge on the spot, but most of the time the rock still gets flung at the bird just to satisfy the curiosity. If the rock hits the bird, which can happen, then there's another throw down of sorts: "bet-cha you killed the bird" which is followed with the "bet-cha I didn't." As you can see, this black and white recreation can keep going and going until supper.

An example of the "I give" form of recreation is the roughest known sport out in any cotton field in the country. Without a doubt, that would be the sport of "cotton trailer football." Please don't get ahead of me because I don't think you know what I am referring to.

Again, let me emphasize there are no rules in rural recreational activities especially in the "I give" category. Cotton trailer football started with my brother and I tromping cotton. You tromp cotton in cotton trailers for two reasons: first, so it won't blow out on the way to the gin, and second, so you can put more cotton in the trailer. Cotton trailers are, for the most part, made of a medium gage wire, and wood that sets on a metal frame. These big rolling containers were around twenty-four feet long, eight feet wide, and eight feet tall. These trailers would hold around 7,500 pounds of fluff. Before going to the gin it took 1,500 pounds of raw cotton to make one bale. A bale weighs in at 480 pounds and that twenty-four foot trailer would accommodate five bales. To take it one step further, when the cotton went through the ginning process there was a little over 1,000 pounds of trash, leaves, and cotton seed separated from the lint that made the bale. Trash went one way, cotton seed went in another direction, and the lint went to the press. Bingo…you got a bale of cotton.

One day, while we were waiting on the cotton picker to dump a load of cotton, we decided to play a game that included me taking off my sock hat and wadding it up in a ball. The person with the ball had four attempts to get it from one end of the cotton trailer to the other end to score. The opponent could keep the offensive person with the ball from scoring by tackling the ball carrier to bring him down.

In order to get a deeper appreciation of this form of recreation, the cotton trailer was made of rough sawn wood that we usually brushed with red paint to distinguish our trailers in the gin lot. With the sun beatin' down on that top board we always got splinters, and, of course, the red paint had lead in it so who knows, we might start talking like Woody Woodpecker during any given minute of our life. There were also metal angle brackets at the center bottom going upward to support the sides of the trailer. When the cotton was topping out on the trailer, you kinda knew where they were but it was generally what we called a WAG (wild ass guess) when covered with cotton. Not to mention you could break your kneecap on one of these brackets when going all out to gain ground.

On one end of the trailer was the tongue used to pull the trailer. The tongue was a piece of steel anywhere from six to eight feet long that was attached to the trailer. The tongue had two welded ends with holes drilled so you could put the pin in to hook-up the trailer to the truck or tractor hitch. This attachment was also a great obstacle to avoid if you went over that end of the trailer. Should you hit the tongue, bones were going to be broken. Totally bad-ass.

You did not keep score as this is without exception an event that ended in one of those bleeding "I give" moments. On a more positive note, cotton was used to soak up blood and did come in handy as this recreation unfolded. This may have been our favorite "I give" recreation in the fall. The sport got better when each of us brought a friend over to play two-on-two. We started taking a couple of round rubber balls up in the trailer because sooner or later one would go out of bounds (out of the trailer) and it was hell going over the side then back up into the arena. It was a good thing that Mom was a nurse because of the jammed fingers that were caught in the wire and bent back, sprains, one chipped elbow, loss of blood, splinters that were just short of wooden arrows, and one nasty eight-foot fall to the ground from the top of the cotton trailer.

We kept Mom up on her continuing education in the nursing field. Hell, I thought someone wrote about her as I saw a book titled "Madam Butterfly" in the school library. My brother and I walked around most of the time with butterfly bandages unless it was a noticeable scar. If there was a need for stitches we usually covered it up with clothing. I bet-cha most of you have never played cotton trailer football.

Another "I give" recreation was burning farts, which usually ended up with a stench of burning ass hair or a second-degree burn on one cheek where the flame shot out. Also beach ball was another game, and I know you're scratching your head asking, "What is so difficult about beach ball?"

Our version of this rural recreational sport was played just like baseball only with an over-inflated beach ball that you hit with a wooden baseball bat. There were no foul lines so when you hit the ball in the air and it caught the wind, it could fly over roads, ditches, railroad tracks, snake pits, or into a telephone pole until it started it descending. If you caught the ball, the batter was out… if you caught the telephone pole, believe me, you were out. Bet-cha would love this game.

Eric and I really did like excitement and when we couldn't find it we made it. I always felt if it weren't for my farm life that that creative side might not have been exposed. At ages thirteen and fourteen we both got fiberglass bows with six target arrows for Christmas presents. The bow had a 25-pound pull. They were lightweight but we figured damage could be done somewhere.

It was a cold Christmas, so the bow and arrow phase was put aside until it got warmer. In the spring, Eric and I finally broke out these new weapons. We both knew how to string a bow but we needed more practice to refine our skill level. After shooting off and on for a week at hay bales, target practice with circles became extremely boring. We needed more fun with a challenge.

What happened next was my idea. "Let's go get the tops of the garbage cans!" I said. In the 60's, these were not made of plastic. Back in the day, they were metal and had a handle on top so that, minus the helmet, you looked just like a gladiator.

I said, "Eric, we'll go across the road into the open field and play chicken."

Eric said, "How?"

"Let's shoot the arrows up straight at the same time and use the garbage can tops as shields. We could play the part of Spartans in battle. We'll see who comes closest." This was kinda death-defying shit, but both Eric and I agreed that an arrow was not goina go through our shield.

Eric liked the idea so we went out on the other side of the road and into a field and started firin' arrows up to see how close it would come to where we were standing. The process was simple: the bows were pulled back at the same time, then on the count of three, we would release the arrows straight up. The safety feature was that it took almost ten seconds before the arrow came back to earth, which gave you plenty of time to defend yourself. We did this with no wind because we didn't want to get one comin' sideways. An arrow in the foot would not be good.

Yep, we were way more than a football field from the front of the house, and we must have shot up fifteen times before Mom's eagle eye looked out the front window. She caught on real quick and came flying across the front yard as we were getting ready to unload another round of arrows into flight. Eric hollered at me then pointed, "Look, Mom!"

We were having fun and Mom had to spoil it. We told her it was safe, the metal garbage can tops were shields, and the wind wasn't blowing. As she was walking us back across the field to the house, she said, "The next time you two pull a stunt like that I'll break those bows." Our mother was strong and we didn't doubt her. She could go off like a firecracker, and we knew Dad was goina get involved, but this time he wanted to try reasoning with us. The reasoning part was much better than the belt. Eric and I both figured that he and his brothers probably pulled the same stunt.

But in the end we all knew that wouldn't last long. We still continued to screw up so Dad continued to take away the more amusing things that we really liked doing. Dad for sure kept up his watch because he knew having our creative side somewhat squashed was going to make life easier for both him and Mom.. From a different view, this just meant more time to dream about those quality opportunities to soon come our way. Eric and I both traded off on a weekly basis of having our asses set on fire. Eric would somehow settle in but I never caught on to the overall plan.

Ok, enough about rural recreation… "I give."

Bet-Cha

Fritz

One night, when I was seven years old and Eric was six, Mom was going about her business of making supper while Eric and I were flippin' channels (all three of them). All of a sudden, Dad perked up and said, "Boys, why don't you go out to the shop and see if y'all can find anything movin'."

We hustled out the back door and towards the shop to find what might be prowling around. The shop was loaded with all sorts of tools, cans of oil and antifreeze, and just about any kind of gadget or gismo to get things done on a farm. You could hide anything in here but for a moment we didn't see anything. Finally we saw these bright eyes starin' at us from under the steel shop table. *Well holy cow*! It was a black and golden-brown puppy that was layin' on the floor with his feet straight out in front, checkin' us out.

I reached in and pulled him out, which was his cue to start acting like a pup. He crawled all over Eric and me, trying to figure us out as much as we were figuring him out.

Later that night, Dad brought up the question, "What are you boys goina name your dog?"

We went through about six names when all of a sudden, Mom spurted out, "What about Fritz? It's a German Shepherd and Fritz is a German name."

Eric and I agreed, and Fritz it was.

This ten-week-old pup would be our companion for the next ten years. As most people may know, a German Shepherd is very protective of his master and Eric and I would become Fritz's masters. Fritz had a nice mix of black and brown colors, just a beautiful coat, very pointed ears when on alert and weighed close to 100 lbs. Plus, he had character that just oozed. He had a slow swagger but eventually would sit down on his haunch in an "I am on ALERT" position that warned people not to mess with his buddies.

We also made him tough by playing lots of games with him. In one of our favorites, we would wrap burlap sacks around our arms and play military attack dog. Eric and I would trade off holding him back by his choke chain collar, then would release him with the command of, "Sic 'em, Fritz." We always had fresh water for him, feed him right, and didn't cut his balls off so he had a good edge on 'em.

Terry Weldon, the infamous 'Pedro' who was the tough wheeling-and-dealing pitcher toeing the rubber when I took my first at-bat, told me of a run-in he had with Fritz. Terry was a sophomore in high school when he went down to see his grandparents in Blytheville, Arkansas, just 50 miles to the south. On his way back, he took a bus to Portageville, Missouri, which was nine miles down the road from our house on Hwy. 162. It was late and close to midnight when Terry decided to try and hitch a ride. He got lucky, and a truck that was heading to Gideon stopped and picked him up.

They drove a ways and before the guy turned down #7 ditch to the south and said, "I gotta let you out here." It was June and the stars were out so Terry put one foot in front of the other, knowing that he was just three miles from his front door.

A half mile down the road was the Littell driveway, and as he was trudging past, all of a sudden something latched onto the back of his butt. *Holy Jesus!*

He could see in the dark that it was a big-ass dog. Terry was now haulin' ass and tryin' to fend the beast off with his duffel bag but the dog got another plug at him. As Terry made it over the bridge, Fritz backed down. But that damn dog let you know his territory and who the hell was boss.

Yep, Fritz would be there at the right time but would also show up at the most unassuming and wrong times as well. He wasn't a hunting dog but could damn well stalk you, plus he could throw out some stealth with that camouflage coat of his.

Since we had cotton in the fields, Dad was always lookin' for ways to cut cost. He'd heard about some farmers down south using geese to weed their fields. Just turn 'em loose in the cotton field and they'd be pullin' weeds and eating 'em. They'd zero in on a weed, then in one stroke with that long neck just snap it up, run it down the hatch, and keep on repeating.

Personally, I'm not really fond of geese. Every time I get within ten feet of one they just light out after me. If you don't make tracks they start makin' that loud honkin' sound, then snap and bite at you with that bill. These weren't little geese either; they were the white ones with the yellow bills, and probably weighed in close to 10 lbs. They were vicious and conniving bastards.

Dad drove all the way down to Kennett, Missouri to pick up twenty-four geese for $2.00 apiece. He drove 'em directly to the cotton field where we had close to eighty acres of cotton that was about six inches high. These guys were there for one purpose—weed control, so Dad cut 'em loose and they went right to work. The field was a half-mile east of where we lived, so the geese were left out there at night where they huddled together until the sun came up and they could go at it again.

The first five days went well. There were less weeds and all the geese were accounted for. They were on a roll. But after a week, Dad came home to tell us over supper that two of the geese had been killed. "It musta been a fox," he said.

The next night, something nailed five of our weed pickers and over the next two weeks we slowly lost the whole flock. The good news was that we found the vicious killer on the day the last goose was taken down. We saw feathers hangin' outta the side of Fritz's mouth. Fritz was now coined a serial killer.

It wasn't his first offense, though. One of our buddies Dale Toole lived down the road and rented our grandparents' house. One cool fall day, we walked down to Dale's house to see if we could stir up some fun or find trouble. We were messing around, and Fritz, who accompanied us everywhere, was sitting on his haunch with ears at full attention and giving us that regal look.

We weren't there a minute when all of a sudden, Dale took a swing and a miss for fun at my head. I immediately said, "Dale, don't do that again," with an elevated voice.

"What you goina do?" Dale taunted.

I said, "Just don't."

As soon as "don't" came outta my mouth, Fritz jumped up at lightning speed and ripped Dale's ear almost off. As Fritz returned to sitting on his haunch, Eric and I could see blood flyin' off Dale's head. *Holy shit, his damn ear was hangin' by a thread!*

We flew to the back door where Mrs. Toole met us and saw the damage. She produced a bunch of towels, and hauled Dale into the car to take him to the hospital.

In my mind I was thinkin', "That's why you don't want to take another swing at me."

Dale told us later that the ear came off on the way to the hospital, but they'd sewed that sucker back on. On the way home, Eric turned to me and said, "He might end up bein' the Van Gogh of the Bootheel."

So now Fritz was a trained assassin as well.

Fritz left our family when I was seventeen. He died in the side yard one morning just before the summer break. If Eric and I were close together and resting on one knee, Fritz would be sitting between us. He was family and took care of us, and we felt fortunate to have had this big playful pup in our lives.

Fritz

Becoming Sparky

You would think by age twelve that one would have a handle on knowing right from wrong. Apparently, I would need more time.

On this particular cold and overcast day in January, my brother and I, along with Carter Fletcher and Dale Toole, were looking to have some fun out on the farm. Dale's family was renting our grandparents' house after we had gotten it cleaned up and ready for someone to occupy. This was where our mom had grown up. There were big sycamore trees in the front yard, a long sidewalk from the house to the mailbox, and to top it off it had a big brick fireplace just off of the front door.

My grandfather was of German decent. He built this house and as kids, my brother and I truly had a lot of fun here, especially if grandma was pissed off at us. Now let it be known that grandma was from some Irish clan. When we started to get a little rambunctious, she pulled out the willow switch. It was something that you didn't want to reckon with, so we got to know all the nooks and tough to reach places. When she got too close we would scurry upstairs. Eventually we would wear her down or wait for grandpa to come through the back door and holler, "Hey boys." Our safe haven had arrived.

Unfortunately my grandparents were killed in an automobile accident in Colorado, but my Aunt Bea was with them and she survived. After that she sort of became our grandma even though she was still Aunt Bea. But more on her later.

Once again, you had to be creative out on the farm to make things happen. Going down the road to the movie show or roller skating when you had that urge to see lights and a different noise was purely a matter of demographics as well as an economics issue. But on this particular Saturday afternoon, Eric and I got well bundled up as we waited for Carter to be dropped off to make the half-mile trek to see Dale.

On my grandparents' death, Mom (an only child) and Dad inherited the farm so Dad took care of the livestock for about six months until they had figured out how to get rid of a herd of 30 cattle, 15 sheep, 40 hogs, 300 chickens, along with guineas, turkeys, and a really big mule. Yeah, it was a real live wild kingdom.

Carter, my lifelong friend, dropped by and we hightailed it down to the house. Dale was lookin' for us and when we got there he came out the back door. Now we were on our big adventure looking for whatever excitement that might come our way. The excitement that we really wanted, though, was toward the barn.

To contain the cattle, Dad decided to put an electric fence around the perimeter of the 30 acres where they grazed. The existing fence was made of old barbed wire that grandpa had put in when he bought the farm way back whenever. The cattle got out several times through this old fence and finally Dad had had enough. The electric fence was easy to put up—it was a single strand of wire that ran through an insulator on a four-foot rod that stuck into the ground about a foot. Encircling the 30 acres was pretty simple, and the cattle now had respect for this little jolt … at least we didn't have to chase 'em down anymore.

That afternoon, we went out to the barn and found the hogs huddled up trying to keep warm. They weighed in around a hundred pounds per hog. I was always extra careful around hogs. My fifth grade teacher Mrs. Shock had told our class about her brother who was playing with a sow's piglets. He was five and got knocked down by the sow. It ate his stomach out before anybody could help, and he bled to death. I was real nervous around hogs after that cautionary tale.

We decided to move on to hopefully bigger and better things. I especially didn't want to fall into the pigpen. With nothing better to do, we decided to walk around the electric fence. We were about three quarters of the way around when one of us decided to take a leak. Well, all the flies went down but I stopped. I wanted to save my stream of pee for something that I thought would be considered a daredevil act.

We walked back up toward the barn where the electrical outlet and fence charger were stuck on a pole, and from there a wire went to the fence. When turned on, the fence was hot. With the fence charger you could set your voltage and surge gap. There was a buzzing sound when the surge was hot and no sound when it stopped, which wasn't for very long. The surge gap was maybe set for one second on, one second off. "Ee-yikes!"

What I was going to do was challenge Eric, Carter, and Dale to piss on the fence on the open gap. Obviously the goal was to miss the hot spot with the current running through it. It was a real challenge, and a small window of opportunity was there for the successor. We could all hear the on-off buzz sound, so listening well was at the top of the list on this challenge.

We weren't playing king of the mountain on this call—this could really knock your pecker in the dirt. I had heard of some people who would just run their electric fence right off the house current. These were the kind of people that would shoot you on their property— not real nice folks, the kind that stay to themselves.

Well it was my idea and yes I was goina go first. I opened my fly, hung 'er out, and started listening for the buzz. I got within ten inches of the wire, never thinking that I would get a full stream on the wire to make contact. My thoughts were on the three other guys. What a hoot.

Well, I was right, my stream of piss hit that fence and nothing happened. Eric decided to get it started and when he moved forward, nudged me into contact with the fence. The current ran right down my pants, but not before it went through my pecker first.

Like Forest Gump says, "Stupid is as stupid does." I went down like a bull elk and in all kinda pain below the beltline. Pecker power was definitely out of the question. Eric and Dale were rollin'. Carter was lookin' down at me shakin' his head, I knew what he was thinkin', "Yeah boy, you be a real dumbass." I had just done Lee's retreat—better yet Lee's surrender. I recovered and made them swear not to tell anybody about this one. It never happened. Just another life lesson. A lightning bolt would most likely kill you, but this was a lesson well learned.

The score: God with a big ONE, zero for Littell.

Cotton picker spindles

Work Daze

When you live out a ways from town, your imagination can run wild. The southeast corner of Missouri is so separate from the rest of the state because the Bootheel was a converted swamp. The land was flat and 99% row crop, some winter wheat, milo, and some corn but mostly soybeans and cotton prevailed.

We needed farm labor, especially when it was time to get the crops outta the field in the fall. Several times we would take a guy just out of the "Big House"; we didn't care, they were troubled men who needed a job and truthfully they were all good workers. They just wanted direction and a job. We didn't care who we took on generally because they got along well with just about anybody. As long as they worked hard and weren't a problem they were welcome.

Whatever the situation or task, each farm hand had his own way of doing things. These guys rubbed off on me and my brother, and we were given a little toughness and kindness to build on from these men who had tough lives. Yes, this part of farm life was a character builder in a positive way. We truly did see and experience, as Johnny Cash would say, the mud, the blood, and the beer.

Jabo

One of the workers was Jabo who was a little flighty but a nonstop guy who wanted to show you he could 'get er done'. I remember very well one day my dad told me to run up to McCord's cotton gin and get Jabo. When we were slow, Dad would always try to find the hired help something else to keep them going, which often meant lending them out to other farmers.

I hopped into the truck and drove up to the gin, pulling around to the side where I thought Jabo might be working. If you've never been in a working gin before— it's LOUD. I walked in and found Jabo working on a section where the lent was separated from the cotton. No seed, no trash, it's ready to go up and through a lot of working parts to get put into bale form at the other end.

I yelled out, "Jabo let's go!"

He yelled back, "Let me finish this. I gotta clean the lent out of this one section."

A gin is super dangerous, with all kind of blades, suction, and the press that hammers cotton into a bale. I was watching Jabo work, getting kind of nervous, so I said, "Jabo, watch out for that blade that comes around it'll cut your hand off."

He yelled back, "I got it timed."

Just as he yelled "timed" the blade came through and cut off three of his fingers.

Blood flew all over and Jabo went down and passed out. I sprinted down to get help, and eventually the ambulance showed up and took him off to the hospital.

Back then, if you had an injury of this magnitude you went into the hospital for a while. After a few days, we heard that Jabo wasn't in the best of spirits because he had tried to commit suicide. But somehow he worked through it.

My dad said when Jabo came back to work not to push him, but let him do the talking. We had a pool table in the office over at the seed shed and about ten days after the accident Jabo walked into where my brother and I were shooting a round of pool. He smiled and said, "Hi, guys, can I play?"

"Well sure, Jabo," I said, looking at his mangled hand that now had just a thumb and a forefinger all wrapped up in gauze. Yee-haw, that looked like it hurt but believe me we most definitely kept a straight face.

To break the ice Jabo went down to shoot and looked up at Eric and me and said, "There's one good thing that came out of this. I now have a slotted slide for that stick to rest on."

We all had a good laugh, and life on the farm went on.

Able

The first guy my dad hired was Able. He was a great guy and a hard worker. He and his wife Pearle Maye lived down the road from us in a shotgun shack, which is made up of three rooms lined up in a row. It was long, so it was coined "shotgun" for the shape. It had one door in the front and one in the back, a porch on the front, with the kitchen being in the back. Eat too many beans and the outhouse was around twenty steps out the back door. The front two rooms were usually bedrooms. If you had four kids, the wife, and the man of the house, well, it got a little close.

Able's day started off like that of any other hard-workin' guy on the farm. Get up at five, throw some clothes on, get something in your gut and go to work. Disc, plow, cultivate, combine, on the cotton picker, hoe, on a tractor all day, the list is endless.

My brother and I loved to hang out with Able. He had a neat gray beard and he could roll a cigarette with one hand. Really cool. One hot day, when I was about five years old, Mom took Eric and me for a walk down to Able's house. The house was right next to a big ditch that had not been cleaned out in a while by the draglines, so there were big trees and brush that were overgrown and just out of hand.

Able told Mom that he was going to go down the ditch a ways to a watering hole where he thought there would be a bunch of water moccasins. Well, my eyes just lit up. "Mom, can I go, can I go?"

Mom agreed, and while she took Eric back to the house, I went with Able on a water moccasin hunt. This was sport for Able. He had a single shot savage .22 rifle and seemed anxious to get out and have some fun.

It had not rained in a while, which was unusual for the Bootheel, so there were isolated potholes of water that moccasins loved. We went just a very short distance and then cut in toward the ditch. We only had to go through about 30 feet of brush and of course, before we went in, Able said, "Mark, try to be quiet."

Able got down on one knee and I watched as he pointed to the watering hole. My eyes got the size of quarters. In this hole of stagnate water I counted out eight water moccasins—bad boys, aggressive, the ones with long fangs. Most were just sunnin' themselves while a couple were swimming' easy through the stagnate water.

Able leveled his savage .22 on the hole and started firin'. That bolt action was moving real fast and he ended up nailing six of the eight. The other two crawled up into the side of the bank. We definitely did not want to go in looking for those guys. Too dangerous. But Able was happy because those things will come up in your yard and hang out around the pump or any wet area. To stay cool they would get under your house and then come out and sun themselves.

Well, my hunt was over, and Able walked me back home where I had plenty of stories for Mom, Dad, and Eric. Nasty things.

Jess

Jess was a strong, good-lookin' black man who came to work on the farm when Eric and I were in junior high. Jess and his wife Everlene had several kids, which was just great for us because we had somebody to hang out with and find trouble.

We did a lot with Jess out on the farm, and spent a lot of time at his house with his two boys Eddie and Larry, who were our age. They both played basketball, Larry played baseball and was also at the top of the list in football, though Gideon football wasn't much. When we needed to have fun we biked down the road to see Eddie and Larry and chop wood, play soldier out in the bean field, or play whiffle ball with a makeshift field.

One of the biggest mishaps we got into was when Dad told Eric and me to get Eddie and Larry to help clean out the pond. That meant we would all get into the shallow end at knee-deep water and start gathering up all the algae we could and throw it up onto the bank. This was a never-ending issue. The pond was a little more than an acre, and it was built on the only gumbo we had on any part of the farm. Gumbo is like clay and it holds water pretty well.

On this particular day, we maneuvered through the bean field about a quarter mile and reached the pond. We took rakes and hoes to try and pull the green gunk up on the bank. There was a shelf on the west side of the pond where we were working that went out about ten feet. But once you went past that, it dropped off and got pretty deep.

It was a hot June day, so we started splashing and kicking water on each other. This cooled us down for a while, but eventually we started throwing this green shit at each other to stir up more fun. Believe me, it could really sting if you got hit by one of these balled-up wads of gunk. At one point, Eddie and I got semi-pissed off at each other, so I picked him up and threw him out over the shelf into the deep water.

He started flailing his arms and yelling, then began to sink.

Larry quickly spoke up and said, "He can't swim."

I said, "What?"

Larry said again, "He can't swim."

Well, my BSA lifeguard skills kicked into gear and I swam out to get him. Eric and Larry helped me pull Eddie back to the bank where he proceeded to throw up. He lay flat in the grass, breathing pretty hard for a while. The fun was over so we trailed back to Eddie and Larry's house and got into some more fun, only this time we were on solid ground.

I asked Eric if he thought I might make it into the papers for savin' a life. He said, "Hell no, but you might have a shot at getting in on attempted murder."

Sonny

When one farm hand moved on Dad would hire another. Sonny appeared kinda fast, but it fit his personality; he was always at the right place at the right time. He was a young, wild guy in his late twenties, and he fit the part. Dad needed a guy on a tractor and a part-time mechanic and Sonny needed some cash. You're hired.

Sonny liked fast cars, fast women, and a little hooch. It really didn't matter which order these vices occurred because in his mind, he had to work to keep it all intact. Over in Portageville there was a circle dirt track and every once in a while we'd drive by and hint to Dad or Mom that this could be a great place to have some real fun. Back in the 60's, there were pretty much no restrictions on what might happen down on the track, the pits, or even in the stands. For $2, country folk could see lots of excitement, for sure a fight, possibly some real blood, and a lot of entertainment. A lot of these folks were 'summer teeth' people…you know, some are here, some are there.

Eric and I got wind that Sonny and his buddy were goina go racin' on Saturday. He had been workin' on the car in the shop after he got finished workin' on the farm. Now, Eric and I had to work on Dad and Mom. We were twelve and thirteen years old, and we put our heads together and determined that we had to do the chores. Feed Fritz on time, weed the garden, mow the lawn, load soybean sacks, all without being told. We thought this might get us some wiggle room when we attempted to negotiate our stance.

Mom and Dad were already onto what we wanted because Sonny was talkin' it up with his buddy Jerry about winning some money over at Portageville at the Saturday night races. Mom and Dad gave in—they would let us go as long as we sat in the stands and not the pits. Done deal, no problem.

We headed over around 5:30, and Eric and I rode in the back of the truck watchin' the car in tow. The trailer was wobbling down the road but we made it. The track was wet that night, as it had rained on Friday, so they were churnin' up the dirt to try and dry it.

We got our tickets and set in the stands. This was what NASCAR was built on—dirt tracks first then the asphalt. We had great seats among the 300 fans waiting for blood. They played the National Anthem and then it was time to race your ass off.

The stands thing didn't last very long, and when the drivers had a break, we scurried down to the pits in the center of the field.

Sonny looked at us and said, "What are you two doin' down here?" He shook his head. "Don't tell your Dad and especially your Mom. Go set on top of that car and stay there unless you see a car comin' straight at you."

We scrambled on top of the car he was pointing at, humming with excitement to be this close to the action. The last part of the race was the best because there was big money on the line. There was some hooch out there in the pits and after the intermission things started to get hot. Guys were shovin' other guys off the track and now they were cussin' up a storm.

During the next-to-last race, a fight broke out in the pits. Sonny and Jerry were taking part, doin' some shovin' and threats were flyin' back and forth. On the last race, these two guys were goin' after each other on the track. It ended up not turning out so well for one of the guys, as his car got hit hard and flipped. The guy that rammed the car stuck his fist out the window shaking it up and down...revenge, you bastard.

The ambulance came onto the track and hauled this guy off to Hayti Memorial Hospital where Mom worked. But the best part was just getting ready to happen, because as the race ended and the cars pull into the infield, three drivers hopped out of their cars and started goin' at each other. It was a knock down drag out and Eric and I had front row seats.

After the races were over, they always shot off about five minutes of fireworks. We definitely got our money's worth that night. When Monday morning rolled around, we got the scoop from Mom about the guy in the wreck. He had to have his spleen removed; minus the mud, the blood and the beer.

Cleo

Cleo was with us the longest. He was a great guy, church-goin' Pentecostal who didn't cuss, drink, or talk about other folks. His wife Ruth and daughters RoSanne and Ruth Anne lived caddy corner from our house. Cleo was always pretty steady with any job that he undertook.

Cleo saved me one time in particular when I had a major malfunction. On this particular day, Dad was P-O'd, so he gave me a job where I couldn't hurt anybody or anything.

He said, "You get your butt on the 930 and go down to the back twenty and disc it up, think you can do that?"

The marine "yes sir" came out of my mouth, crystal clear. I turned around and headed for the tractor. I wasn't goina give him the chance to say, "Now get goin'."

The 930 was a tractor that pulled a twenty-one foot disc. It was wide and could run deep into the dirt. I traipsed down the back road and pulled it into the field. My very first thought when I pulled in was, *I've got to do a hell of a job to get back on top of Dad's good list.*

I started on the east side and worked towards the west. There was one really big cypress tree smack dab in the middle of the field that had weeds growin' up around the trunk. I thought I would get up close with the disc and make it look real pretty. I got to the middle and was going through the field in third gear high with that big diesel, black smoke flyin' because I was runnin' deep. I cut through the field at an angle to get to the tree and I just clicked it up a notch to full throttle. I was moving fast around the tree, going back and forth getting within a couple of feet of the trunk. I thought I could do better, and get it trimmed up real fine. Four more passes and I would have done such a hell-of-a job, maybe I would get off of Dad's shit list.

On the third pass toeing this twenty-one foot disc, I got a little too close and my back disc blade hit the tree. The momentum from the tractor going forward shot the disc about five feet up the trunk, just enough to pull the tractor tires off the ground and just spin. It caught me off-guard as I shut the tractor down pronto. I had both a disc and a tractor up in the air, the front tires were down on the ground, half the disc was up the tree, and the whole thing looked like a piece of art.

I climbed down and stepped back to assess the situation. If my assessment was right, my ass was in trouble… again. I was three quarters of a mile away from the house and shop where the other tractor was, so I started haulin' ass across the field. I got back to the shop where Cleo was. As soon as he saw me, he said, "What's wrong, boy?"

I caught my breath, panting as I tried to catch some air. I started talkin' like Tarzan, "Tractor up tree…tractor in tree…got to get down…need help…need chain. Dad, no ass, no ass, need help Cleo."

I went over to hydrate and doused my head under the faucet. I finally started to come to my senses and bless Cleo, he was walking through the shed carrying a chain as I heard another tractor cranked up. Yep, we were goina go pull that monstrosity out of the tree.

Cleo brought around the 720 John Deere. I put my foot on the hitch and held on to the back of the seat and we were off. When we pulled up to this disastrous event, Cleo sized it up, shaking his head. "How'd you get it up and into the tree?"

"It wasn't easy," I said. How about, "I be a dumbass!"

We hooked up the tractor to the disc and managed to pull this thing out of the tree. Once it was out, Cleo looked at the disc and alignment and said, "I think you got lucky. Doesn't look like the disc is bent. Start it back up and make a run through the field."

I did and neither the tractor nor disc pulled either direction so I felt that the monkey had just come off my back.

"The field looks great, by the way," Cleo said with a laugh, as he headed back to the shop.

Later that evening, Dad said, "You did a nice job on that back twenty."

Yes sir, clean as a whistle.

Cleo was cool. He saved me and didn't say a word to Dad. I thought I got off clean and clear until six months later when all four of us were setting around the table at Christmas, playing cards and having hot toddies. We were into the card game and Dad said, "Mark, your card playin' is getting better. Matter of fact, I think it's better than when you disc a field."

"Hey, Dad," I said. "I take pride in the way I disc up a field. I clean up everything."

"Well, how about the time you ran the tractor and disc up the tree on that back twenty?" He started laughing at my shocked look, and added, "I watched the whole thing from the house. I just wanted to see how you were going to handle this one. You did well."

Can't win them all, but at least I still got my ass intact.

My Brother and I
"Lead" a MLK March

Well, Mom had a "Mom" moment. We had all just sat down to have supper one Wednesday evening in March of 1968, and our Mom decided to announce her presence to me and my brother.

"Boys, we're going to go to Goldsmith's tomorrow to do some shopping."

Goldsmith's in the 60's was touted as the greatest store in Memphis and, of course, my Dad was rolling his eyes for two reasons: one, because he knew that Eric and I were not going to be cultured country boys and would probably find trouble or create some mischief in the big city of Memphis, and two, because without a doubt Mom was going to spend money on some really weird shit for the house, yard, or to make me and Eric look real stupid at school. Mom used to buy these clothes for us that matched. Sometimes we looked like two orange vans comin' at ya. We didn't know what peer pressure was but both of us knew how to throw a punch to the nose.

All I knew was that we had better things to do than drive an hour and twenty minutes down then back just to be bored in a huge department store. The escalators were the only fun part because we could burn off that pent-up energy and play "You're It." Hopefully we wouldn't run into the store security guy who was basically Barney Fife minus the bullet. The second best thing to look forward to, without a doubt, was eating Memphis barbeque. After burning through the escalators, trying on a few bras and flippin' ladies pants at each other, we figured we were due for food. We needed nutrition and Memphis had the best. We decided we were goina give Mom two hours and then start whinin'.

At this time, I was a ninth grader and Eric was a year behind. It was a Wednesday and on Thursday and Friday there was a teacher's conference for most of the teachers in the Bootheel. I guess they needed to confer about the education they were spreading. I didn't care because hum baby it meant no school!

This Thursday would end up being a very special day, it just hadn't come to fruition yet. All we knew was that we were going to miss out on some rat-killin' in the morning, starting a fire to burn off the ditches in the afternoon, and going to Gemberling's thicket. The thicket was twenty acres of unmolested woods that had an Indian mound right smack dab in the middle— spooky, but fun. When we played in the thicket, we came in from the south so we always had to pass by the Hilfiker Bee Hives. There were usually twenty hives set out in this very active corner tucked away where these bees could do their job. Jamer Hilfiker was the son and was about four years older than me. He was always telling us bee stories at school. On our way in we would get close to the hives but never got stung. At the time these hives had no African bees—they were the nice ones.

But instead of having those adventures, we got up the next morning at 6:30 am to make the drive to Memphis. Dad had breakfast ready and we finally peeled out of the farm at 7:30 sharp. Mom said she wanted to get to Goldsmith's at 9:00 to get a jump on the crowds because, "Not everybody has a teacher's conference going on to offset those big store sales."

On this Thursday, March 28th, we had a feeling that it was going to be very quiet in the big city. But we would soon be proven wrong. We rode down in this big Mercury "country squire" station wagon; it's the one that has the fake wood panel siding that runs the length of the huge boat of a car, but under the hood it had a big 390 engine that could kick butt when needed. We took our pillows, knocked down the middle seats and had more than six feet to scamper around in and plenty of room to snooze.

Mom got down to Memphis in plenty of time. She had a lead foot and a few tickets to show for it. Johnny Rutherford was a distant cousin on Mom's side, and Dad always said she tried to emulate the Indy winner. I really think she would have fit in much better at the Bonneville Salt Flats rather than Interstate 70.

Before we crossed the bridge over the Mississippi River, you couldn't help but notice that Memphis stood out—just a great skyline coming in from the west. The sun was up and Elvis was probably having a snooze after an all-night "Bible Study." The only time I ever saw Elvis was when we were driving by his mansion when I was ten years old. Dad was driving and Mom looked up and said, "Look, boys. Elvis is out front with his cars."

These cars included a jeep with a red and white candy cane top and a pink Cadillac. To the King, I guess this was cool.

We drove down Main St. and made it to Goldsmith's. There was barely a soul in sight as we entered the indoor parking lot. One of the really fun things about going to Goldsmith's was the ride up or down on the car "round-about" to get to your designated floor, or one that wasn't full. Yes siree, we weren't leading a sheltered life. Memphis and St. Louis were meant for parking the masses. So was Gideon, but you had to go up in the big city and not out on the flats so much.

We rode the round-about all the way to the top and parked upstairs—mission accomplished. We walked into Goldsmith's a little after nine o'clock. Now Mom could go do her thing and Eric and I could do ours. In a matter of five minutes, we had gone up to the top floor and were trying to figure out if there was any fun in this store.

Time passed and eventually Eric and I grew bored. We had already been run out of the women's department for trying on the bras and had as much fun as we could on the escalators. Around 10:15, this Southern woman's voice came over the store intercom. She was really calm but we knew this voice carried weight and that there was a qualified person on the other end of this mike.

This was much better than the PA system at the Gideon high school. This was Elvis's territory, after all.

The voice carried a message: "We would like everyone to proceed to the exits calmly. At this time there is a Martin Luther King, march coming down Main Street and it's heading toward Goldsmith's."

People were now getting a little crazy while our Mom was more than a little hysterical. Frantic, might be a better word. So much for being calm, cool, and collected. And yes…my brother and I were having a blast. We were going to witness history.

We found the car in our best ever time. I knocked the seat down in the middle of the station wagon. I did not, repeat, did *not* want to miss a single drop of this excitement. Eric headed to the back and was all scrunched up, but he made do as Mom jerked outta the lot like Johnny Rutherford pullin' out of a pit stop.

We always got the Memphis Commercial Appeal, and Dad always kept up with what was going on in the city, but this one demonstration came out of nowhere. It went bad fast and a lot of people were put in harm's way. This was not Ken and Barbie territory; it was time for Action Jackson.

The march started over the strike of black sanitation workers. There was a boycott as they sought job safety, better wages, benefits, and union recognition. Memphis was one of the more noteworthy battlefields where King and his followers fought for equal rights. Seven days later, Martin Luther King Jr. was shot and killed at the Lorraine Motel, a place Eric and I were very familiar with. Dad would ask us to take down a load of soybeans to Memphis in our two-ton truck to be dumped on the barge where these soybeans were sold to be made into oil. When we dumped beans, we drove right below the Lorraine Motel, and we would always stop nearby for barbeque for nourishment before that haul back to the Missouri line.

Getting back to the action, we went down the round-about and it was much more fun this time as Mom was moving faster. The tires were screeching and the shocks had to have taken a beating. Seeing a mass of pissed-off people could be exciting, but Mom was going to keep her two boys safe and in check at all costs. As we got to the bottom of the lot, there was a line of cars heading down the street towards the Mississippi River. We should have been going to the left, but when we looked up the hill to the right there weren't any cars going east toward Main Street.

Well, Mom did Pickett's charge, and went right on the side street. (Pickett's charge was an infantry assault directed at Union positions on Cemetery Ridge on July 3rd, 1863 during the Battle of Gettysburg. The

Confederates would end up losing over half of their men in this decisive battle.) I know she was thinking that she would out-maneuver everybody. Eric and I were being loud and laughing and having fun. We looked at each other, not saying a word but thinking, "What the hell is Mom doin?"

Mom had her head down searching for WMPS to get more information about the march. She was fidgeting with the radio as she crept forward to take a right onto Main Street. This was good as there were no cars, just a wide-open street. Our mother was mumbling out loud, "Where is this march going?" Then she turned and said to us, "Boys, be quiet I'm trying to find out where this march is going."

My brother opened his mouth and I will always remember his next line: "Hey, Mom, you're leadin' it!"

Just to the left of the car was a wall of pissed-off black folks. We turned around to see Eric waving to the mass of people in this march now turned riot, which was less than a hundred feet behind us. Retailer storefronts, windows, and doors were being broken and shattered, cars were hammered, and big time problems were now in effect.

There used to be a law that you couldn't honk your horn in Memphis, or you would get a fine. This uprising would surpass the horn honkin' law. That day we learned what "putting the pedal to the medal" truly meant. The Big Merc kicked into passing gear and smoked down Main Street. The fun was over. We had led the march for less than twenty seconds before Mom was racing us out of there.

To make it worse, we ate barbeque on the Arkansas side. Their hog is good, but compared to Memphis barbeque...well, there is no comparison. We got back to the farm and immediately told Dad about all the ruckus. All we got out of him were three eyerolls. As far as the trip went, I figured that, other than Bobby Kennedy, Eric and I might be the only two white boys to lead a MLK march. Making history was some kinda fun.

My Brother and I "Lead" a MLK March

DDT—What A Wonderful Word

Dichlorodiphenyltrichloroethane was good stuff. It would kill just about anything. One might say that I was one of the true survivors of this chemical. Better known as DDT, my exposure to this substance probably helped contribute to my position as a closer at the Big League level. I have always said that to operate at that optimum level, one would need an IQ of around 3 to 5. When coming in to pitch the 8th or 9th inning,

I just knew I had that needed edge—just point me to the mound.

Spraying DDT and all of these other concoctions of doom let off such a smell. They would kill any creepy crawler that landed in our fields. Another chemical that was my favorite was cotton defoliant. This was an off shoot of "Agent Orange." What a great fragrance! My nostrils would flare and my eyes would roll back just like Anthony Hopkins in *Silence of the Lambs*. A cotton defoliant's job was to knock the leaves off the cotton stalk so the bolls could be exposed to the sun. Once unprotected from the sun, the bolls of cotton could open up faster, thus speeding up the process of getting the cotton out of the field sooner.

When Round Up came out it did a great job of takin' the weeds out. Of course, it too had a great smell since its base was soap, which made it stick to the plant. The only thing I didn't like about Round Up was the taste; it made ya pucker.

To get these chemicals into the field fast, we would hire a crop duster to spray it on with planes that were reeved up to carry a big load of water mixed with chemicals. If we were spraying near our house, Dad had us put the horses in the barn, and Eric and I would go in and stay with 'em. We'd be blowin' our air into their nostrils to calm 'em down. We didn't want Princess or Firecracker suckin' in much of that inhospitable brew.

The planes they used to distribute the chemical were magnificent, and I used to be a flag boy (a human marker) for a couple of crop dusters, better known as flyboys. Without a doubt these crop dustin' guys were nuts—pure daredevils. They loved it, doing maneuvers and tactics that were outta sight. I marveled at their loop-t-loops, drop down or pull 'er up, and get the hell outta dodge mode.

I'd watch and my brain just clicked into overdrive ... did I just see what I thought I saw? They would fly under a telephone line that was on the other side of the road when you knew damn well they could have pulled up sooner. Then they'd wave at you with the tail of the plane after they passed to show off their swagger. Or they dropped down through a pecan grove to get to the field so they could pick up and keep the line on the next run.

These guys clicked along between 90 to 95 MPH and with precision timing. They would dump a load (the chemical) then move up while shutting off their tanks. Then they would circle around and make the turn for the next pass.

My job as a marker was to count off the needed steps so the spray could touch the outside row. I usually took twenty-four steps to get the flyboy back in line for that next pass, then it was his job to hold the plane straight for the length of the field. The really cool thing is that this plane would move through the field at twelve to fifteen feet off the ground. It's a beautiful sight to see especially when it's coming right at you with a shower of chemical raining from its underbelly.

One of the more fun things for me to do when I was really bored was to pick up small rocks on the road, about the size of a marble. When the plane came over low enough with no telephone lines on the other side of the road I'd flip this rock up at the propeller, trying to hit it to see where it would go and the sound it might make. When it hit the propeller the rock made just a really cool sound … ZINGGGGG.

There are two reasons I eventually cut this shit out. John Huie, who owned and flew these magnificent planes, chewed my ass out one day. I would usually go back to the airport to help him load the chemicals in the tank. That's when he yelled, "Mark, get over here" in a not-so-good tone. "I want to show you something."

I stood next to him by the plane and looked where he pointed. "You see this propeller? You see those nicks in the propeller? Well, I don't think you can afford to buy me a new propeller blade."

Just like a derelict I was shaking my head up and down going north to south. Yep, John was pissed.

"And another thing. You've heard that 'ZINGGGG' sound when it comes off the blade? That rock is now a projectile and will go right through your body."

The truth was out. He too had done this, but what a great sound. I stopped because I didn't want a hole in my head, though some people had already told me I had a hole in my head.

John Huie was a true daredevil who flew in World War II. He had wonderful planes: a two-winged Stearman and a single-winged Pawnee. The Pawnee was yellow and sleek but the Stearman made this great sound that just rumbled through your body.

When you marked for a plane, you wore a raincoat because at the end of the day you were the color of the chemical being dropped. I ended up being bright yellow or just a clear coat. But it did smell great. Mom would always yell at me to get into the shower and scrub up good, then she'd light into Dad's ass for letting me be a marker. I was really glad to be in the shower when Dad was catching the short end of the stick from Mom; she could be vicious.

Hell, one of these days in my golden years I might just start singing "Tip Toe Through The Tulips" like Tiny Tim, minus the ukulele and tulips, then finish on a roll by reciting the Missouri State Driver's Manual.

Dynamite Daze

*E*ric and I sure did have a good time out on the farm, but when something was dangerous it just upped the ante. Danger meant livin' in the fast lane.

It was June and school had been out for a couple of weeks. I was fifteen and it was going to be a hot summer, as always. Playing American Legion ball over at Poplar Bluff was almost an everyday affair in the summer. From time to time, our team would take a trip across the river into Kentucky, or go down and play some teams in Arkansas or Tennessee, or even make it up to St. Louis and wrangle some of the teams up north. But back on the farm, the chores never stopped for me and Eric. You would think we couldn't have gotten into too much trouble, as busy as we were. But somehow, the Gruesome Twosome still managed to find mischief, which usually boiled down to trouble.

In the mornings, Dad would mostly have us do tedious crap. First thing we'd do was go into the shop. We might change out the old cultivator points for new ones (remember, back then we had wrenches—no fancy-ass pneumatic tools). Then we'd go into the fields and churn up the ground—loosen it to let the roots spread. It didn't matter if it was corn, cotton, or soybeans (and let it be known that New Madrid County was *big* on soybean production). If we hadn't set one of the cultivator points right, and it was "off" when it went into the ground, we'd hear about it—we'd definitely hear about it.

At other times, when it was dry with dirt and the dust was thick when disking the fields, we'd change out or clean the air filters on the tractors. Keeping the engines clean was a priority. We had to make sure everything was running smooth, which we usually did before dinner (lunch). We had a dinner bell but it didn't need to be used. We'd eat anything that was dead and had the hair knocked off.

One thing we did *not* like to do was clean out the garden. This was just another dull and boring chore.

Mom would chime out, "Make sure to get all those weeds out, boys!"

"Yes, Mom."

"Make sure to get enough water on the end row!"

"No problem, Mom."

The only good thing about the garden was that we always did it barefooted. Yes siree, it was cool and squishy, and it was a quite-pleasing feeling to have that good Bootheel dirt moving in between your toes.

The *really* hard job was when it was ninety degrees and someone showed up with a two-ton truck, needing two or three hundred bushels of soybeans. A bushel sack weighs in at sixty pounds. That could be unforgiving. The soybean shed was all tin, and the humidity, as always, could be cut with a knife. As a general result, Eric and I would be at least *half* pissed-off by the time some good ole boy from Arkansas pulled up to the seed shed. Most could barely talk—some even grunted. And if we weren't already bent out of shape, this would sure do the trick. This inbred would be eatin' a moon pie and smokin' a cig in his left hand, and suckin' down an RC Cola in his right. He'd be sitting on a pallet of stacked soybeans, snickering, "Can't y'all hurry up?" with all kinds a shit runnin' down the side of his mouth. *Get yourself a napkin, moron.*

But one job my brother and I really *did* like was when Dad was blowin' a stump with dynamite. He would always let us in on the action. It was amazing to see how much sheer *damage* a few sticks of dynamite could do when positioned in the right place. In the Sixties, dynamite was easy to get; just walk into the hardware store, show 'em your driver's license, sign a form saying you're not a felon, lay down fifty dollars, and then swing around back and they'd load you up with a case of real *panther piss* (hot stuff). We would go to the hardware store over at Portageville and get all the goodies: dynamite, blasting caps, cord, large auger, small auger—hell, we were ready. We'd load the dynamite into the truck bed and put the blasting caps in the glove box—yes, it was *extremely* important to keep the dynamite and the caps separate. Should the caps be settin' in the same box as the dynamite and get jarred...*sayonara*. There'd be nothing left but four smoking wheels and a considerably bent-up frame.

Dad was blowing a lot of stumps up at Momma Sally's house in "Tally" (Tallapoosa). He opted for dynamite over a bulldozer because of the cost factor— heavy equipment could get pricey. Also, there was another factor to consider: when the dynamite obliterated a stump, all we had to do was pick up the scattered chunks and throw 'em into the trailer for firewood—no chainsaw, no choppin', done deal.

Eric and I knew we had this stump-blowing figured out. We wanted to blow one of these humongous oak stumps ourselves, so we mapped out a plan to ask Dad at the right time. We worked steady for a couple of days, staying out of trouble, and finally built up enough nerve to sit down and ask. After we finished with supper, I leaned forward and asked, "Dad, can Eric and I go blow a stump on our own?"

He paused, then responded, "I'll let you two go up to Tally and blow a stump if you promise me that once you've fired up the line (dynamite cord), you *will not* cut it. Any problems … just let it blow."

"Oh, Dad, we promise, you bet! We'll get it done and make sure everything is in order—we got a plan."

"Well, all right. Tomorrow, you two can head up to Tally and get rid of one of the big oak stumps."

Hum baby, were going to do some demolition, clear the land, make room for more soybeans, straighter rows, productive and proactive—yep, Eric and I were getting our shit together!

We were anxious and woke up early the next day, had breakfast, and started loading up the faded red 1959 International pickup. Almost everything on our farm was of International Harvester make, except for a couple of steady 'n reliable John Deere tractors. (We also acquired a 930 Case tractor when I was a sophomore—we put doolies on the rear wheels so it could pull through just about anything.) The '59 International was basically a tank with a 304 V8 engine. It was built strong and held steady but it rode like a bull. The three-speed tranny could pull big loads, yet only cruise at about sixty-five miles an hour. It was a lug. I sure hoped that I wouldn't have to take *this* out on a date when I turned sixteen—it was butt-ugly and definitely *not* a chick magnet.

Dad was keeping an eye on how we were loading up the truck and said, "Looks like you boys are ready. Have you got matches?"

Well, kiss a duck's red ass, how could we forget matches? I ran into the house and got a whole box of kitchen matches, at least a couple hundred ("Be prepared"—Boy Scouts' motto). We filled up the truck with gas and waved "goodbye" to Dad, then stuck our thumbs up as added assurance. Cleo, who worked for us, yelled, "Git 'er done!" Fritz, our German Shepherd and trusty companion, would have to stay at the house on this one because we didn't want him going ape-shit when the explosion went off. A dog's ears are sensitive and there was no need to push it—he was our buddy.

I drove east for around five miles and made the turn off on the 162 and swung north along the floodway toward Tally. We stopped by to see Momma Sally, and grab anything that wasn't tied down and looked good enough to eat in the kitchen. "You boys be careful with that dynamite. If not handled right, it's flat-out dangerous," she warned. Well, we were just thinking how lucky we were to be in such a risky and unsafe position. This was bold daredevil shit.

We drove up and parked the truck about fifteen feet from the biggest stump in the field. It must have been forty inches across and was sticking up almost three feet out of the ground. We dropped the truck bed and started throwin' out almost everything. We drew the line on throwing the dynamite though. We reached for the big auger, which was three inches in diameter and could go down almost four feet. It had a wooden handle on top for you to latch onto when you turned it into the ground—pure grunt-work. Our plan was to put down three holes that would form a triangle around the base of the tree. We would angle them towards the center to concentrate the charge.

The holes were dug—then the fun began. We removed the case of dynamite from the truck. The case was a little over half full, which was more than we'd need—definitely enough firepower for a hell of a show. We brought out the roll of bright-orange dynamite cord, which was about the size of your little finger, and took the blasting caps and small auger out of the glove compartment. The caps reminded me of the Lone Ranger's silver bullet. Too bad Tonto couldn't make this trip.

I picked up a stick of dynamite and said, "Eric, how many turds should we throw down the hole?" We called 'em "turds" because they were around twelve inches long, two-and-a-half inches in diameter, and wrapped in brown wax paper. Giant turds = giant damage. Dad told us to put in twelve sticks of dynamite (four down each hole), but we were determined to make this monster of a stump come out *fast* with no glitches. So, we decide to put *six* turds into a hole—a total of eighteen for the stump. A little drama? Maybe.

The last stick of dynamite was the charge. Starting on the side in the center of this turd of magic, you would punch in three holes about three inches apart to set things in place. This Lone Ranger of a cap was pressed into the middle hole, then the cord was pushed through one side out the hole and back down and through the other outer hole. Then, as the cord burned down and touched the cap ... hum baby! Ignition then fireworks.

With this stick of doom all doctored up, it was ready to be put into place. We pushed it down the last hole already loaded with the five other turds. When you put this stick of doom down the hole, you pushed it to the bottom using a shovel handle. You wanted them snug against each other. You controlled the handle with your hands on the blade, and barely, and I mean barely, tap the doom stick into place.

At this juncture you would see about three feet of this orange dynamite cord coming out of the ground—it was pretty. We covered up all the holes, stepped back, made eye contact and nodded. Yep, it's a done deal.

You're probably wondering how we measured for time. The dynamite cord would generally burn at one minute per foot measured. We measured out five feet for five minutes of time to get our asses out of the way. We felt safe and there was no clear and present danger.

Eric and I threw all the tools and what was left of the dynamite into the truck bed and closed it up. The blasting caps went in the glove compartment while I pushed up some more dirt around the last hole.

Eric was on the other side of the truck and I hollered, "Are we ready for a *fire in the hole?*"

"Yep, light it!"

The match was struck.

One other item we each brought was our Timex watches, so that as soon as we lit the fuse, we could gauge *to the second* just how long we had 'till the big bang. So I glanced at the watch that "takes a lickin' and keeps on tickin'." Eric was settled in the passenger's seat and I jumped into the truck. The truck started and I shoved it into first gear, hoping to gain some *relatively safe distance between the stump and us. Maybe a hundred yards or so should get us clear…but we did throw in six more sticks…eighteen big brown turds should flush out this chunk of wood…*

Well, I shoved it into first gear and hit the gas—but the back wheels just spun and the rear end started to sink a little. *Well shit a brick.* I shoved it into reverse to see if we could just back out this big hunk of metal. I hit the gas pedal easy and the truck moved just a touch, but it sunk even further. I pushed the panic button, rammed it into first gear again, and hit the pedal hard. But the back tires just spun as the truck kept sinking. I turned off the truck—the cord was burning steady—and looked at Eric and said, *"Holy shit,* we gotta exit…*fast."*

We left everything and ran out less than fifty yards or so. We settled in on one knee to watch the show, but our thoughts weren't really on the explosion of the stump—we were mostly thinkin' 'bout what Dad was goina do to us. We would be minus an ass the next morning. We were still checking our watches and counting backwards—*"Twenty-five seconds and it's gonna blow!"*

"No—twenty!"

What really mattered was how much damage was gonna be done to that big red mass of metal setting fifteen feet away from eighteen *very* hot turds ready to slam into the driver's side.

One thing about dynamite: it doesn't just go "boom"—it can *roar*. Yep, for a second and a half, the ground we were standing on *rattled*. Then the fireworks started. You could almost feel every stick go off. From the tremor of the ground shaking to the detonation then the explosion, some real serious damage was quite evident. My hearing was perked as I heard torn-away pieces of the oak stump slamming into the side of the truck. My head was moving side to side fast, trying to keep up with all the big loose chunks of oak floating through the air. I could see the glass being removed from some of the windows—"blown out" is probably a better way of putting it. It was all very exciting for about five seconds, just like a movie ... but then it was back to reality. This reality was the fact that Eric and I *weren't quite far enough* from ground zero. Little pieces of splintery wood and dirt were flying into our space (even with the truck between us and the stump) and soon we were both covered with fine, granular bits of dirt, with some remains of fragmented oak wood stuck on our t-shirts.

Holy shit—we ran to check out the damage. From seventy-five feet out you could see only partial damage to the vehicle. All the windows were just crumbs of safety glass scattered on the hood and on the ground. We got closer, and we saw that the back window had "survived," but there was a horizontal crack running the full length of the glass but the shotgun rack was still in place This wasn't going to impress Dad, and we seriously doubted that there would be *any* negotiation on *any* of the damage.

We walked around to the driver's side to check out the real damage, but before looking at the truck we just couldn't help but glance at the hole in the ground…at least five feet deep and twelve feet across. Hey, good news…the stump was gone. But turning back and looking at the driver's side of the truck was a different story. Let's just say it was kinda like lookin' at modern art. Yes, the damage was "out there." Really out there. It was crumpled, wrinkled, crushed, uneven, rutted—even the damn door was jammed shut.

With all the chunks of oak stump lying around, we had no problem getting the red International tank to move; some shovel work and the placement of the scattered oak under both wheels eventually freed the rear end as we moved forward. We loaded up and got out of the field fast. There was just no need to stop to say "goodbye" to Momma Sally (we didn't want her to call Dad and give him a heads-up that we had blown off half the truck). The windows bein' blown out slowed us to around fifty miles per hour, but we made it back to the house and drove in toward the shop. For some reason, Dad was in the shop even though he was hardly ever out there. My brain went into overdrive as Eric stayed calm as a cucumber because he knew it was my ass that was goina be in the sling.

At this moment I was now in "clear and present danger." Thinking quickly, I realized I was lined up to drive in on the good side…Eric's side. For the time being this was a good thought. Also, I parked far enough away so Dad wouldn't figure out that it wasn't Windex making these windows so clear.

I decided to park out a ways by the gas tank as I swung Big Red around. Eric got out as I was trying to come up with an exit plan. I heard Dad say to Eric, "How'd it go? You guys get rid of that stump?"

"Well, we got 'er out, but we kinda got a problem," Eric was fumbling for words, as I was lying flat on my back trying to kick open the driver's door from the inside. I finally gave up, crawled out the passenger's side, and faced the fiddler. Dad was so numb with brain disease setting in fast that he was at a loss for words. We were stupefied—we hadn't ever seen this reaction outta Dad before. Finally, we explained the whole process, and without saying anything he went inside to either contemplate the damage or get a gun. Maybe he was in awe as to how much damage was done to this trusty red beast of a truck.

Surprisingly, not too much happened to us. Dad must have also been amazed at how much damage eighteen sticks of dynamite could stir up—uh, I mean twelve. For the first time ever, Dad went out and bought an off-breed: a '67 Chevy truck. We were normally Ford folks, but the small block 327 engine under that hood would absolutely haul ass. We could wax this one, and it was even a good date truck.

Coon Huntin'
and Coon Cookin'

My grandfather Littell loved to coon hunt. In fact, the whole Littell Clan liked this particular sport. My granddad Littell died when I was one year old, but that didn't stop me from going after that masked bandit.

To go out and git 'em you always want to have a good coonhound or hounds, a .22 rifle, and a real good flashlight or head lantern; this would get you into the woods. Coons were all over the Bootheel, and if you found one in the barn or in the trash he was goina end up on the table, with our family, anyway.

Finding a good coonhound was sometimes tough. There are a lot of breeds, including black and tan, tree walkers, blue tick, and the list goes on. The prettiest sound in the woods was to hear a bunch of hounds on the trail of a coon. On a rare occasion, you might hit the mother lode and get three or four into one tree. It was a pretty sight to see.

But it really didn't matter if you had one up the tree or five; these hounds were on the hunt and going berserk. When you shot one and it fell, you had to hold the dogs tight because you didn't want a chewed-up coon, or worse, a chewed-up hound. Coons were vicious bastards. I had one cornered in a barn out in Kansas when I was pitching for the Royals. This hay barn was full of coons. The barn belonged to John Town, who I used to hunt with all over two or three states when the off-season rolled around. John didn't want me to take a rifle into the barn, and for good reason; he didn't want any holes in the walls. So I picked up a hay hook and figured that would be my weapon of choice. The coon saw me and I ran him into the corner. I really thought this thing was goina go up and over me. I hung that hay hook right in front of his face and he swatted at it, almost knocking it out of my hand. This pissed me off so I just smoked him behind the head, and said, "I win."

We skinned him and John took the pelt and I took the meat. He couldn't believe I was going to eat this critter. Coon is good eatin'—its dark meat is tender when fixed right. I used to go out with this girl from Campbell, Missouri, who had a pet coon that was calm for the most part. I just didn't want him to start gnawing on me. I drew the line when she got the pet skunk. I'm outta here.

Coon season was from the middle of November 'til the end of January when it got cool out there. One of the best places to hunt in the Bootheel was the bar pits on the Mississippi River. The bar pits were formed from the levee that was built. These humongous draglines and bulldozers pulled up dirt to form the levee that would hold back the river and keep the Bootheel from flooding. It was a swamp. It had high and low spots but the water depth was around six feet—good for fishing. The bar pits were filled with crape and catfish, and of course, lots of water moccasins. But the coon huntin' was real good.

When you hunt at the bar pits, there's a chance you could lose a dog. My granddad did. He had a hound on a coon and the coon went into the water and the dog followed. The dog was just about to get him when the coon turned, got on top of the dog's head, drowned the dog and escaped. A tragedy.

Another way to hunt these guys is by mule. A mule will go through just about anything while a horse gives you little to no effort; they're not as smart as a mule. Horses will not go through limbs or jump over obstacles. Mules are great, steady and true. They just fart a lot.

When I was home during the off-season, I needed to go up to the IGA in Gideon. My sweet tooth was not sweet so I felt like ice cream would solve the problem. It was late, around ten o'clock, and I cranked up the '71 Merc with the 390 in it. It moved and so did I. It was nothing to go 90 MPH in the Bootheel as the roads were straight, nobody was on them, and the speed limit was 75 MPH. If you went 15 or 20 over, no big deal. I put the pedal down and got her crankin'. I crossed #5 ditch and rounded the curve. I punched it going toward #4 ditch. The #4 ditch came up fast, and I hit the front of the bridge as the car jumped off the end and landed straight. A hundred yards down the road, a coon ran right out in front of the Merc. In a flash, he was road kill. I stopped and threw him in the trunk, went up and got some ice cream, and at 10:30 I was skinning a coon. Eric was off to college, and I wanted to surprise Mom and Dad with a coon super the next day. It was a 7 or 8-pound coon, a young one so this was going to test my kitchen skills. I baked him and it turned out great. How can you screw up cooking a coon?

Our German Shepherd Fritz even got in on the action one night. Mom was the one who really got it going when she just started yelling up a storm. "Alan, Alan, there's a dog up the pole! Fritz has a dog up the pole."

In the backyard we had a garden, a windmill, a 500-gallon LP tank and a farm light that lit up just about everything that was on this telephone pole. Eric and I were wide awake and peeking into their room to see what all the commotion was about. Heck, I'm deaf in one ear and Mom even tore me away from my sleep. Dad got out of bed and looked out and said, "Hell, Jeanne, that's not a dog that's a coon."

Now Eric and I started howlin' as Dad reached for the .22 rifle. He did not want to miss out on a Sunday coon dinner. He maneuvered around and out the back door. The dog, I mean the coon, and Fritz were gone, but you can bet that Fritz was on this coon's ass. I hoped he wouldn't get scratched up too bad. We went back to bed with visions of a dog clinging to a telephone pole dancing in our heads. We woke up the next morning and found Fritz with just a few scratches on his muzzle and some blood on his ear. He was rearin' to go but Mom was taking some heat for reporting the dog-up-the-pole incident. She was cooking breakfast when Eric and I sat down.

Dad said, "Jeanne, I saw this coon driving a tractor this morning."

Eric turned to me and said, "I saw one humpin' a mailbox."

Yeah, Mom had her hands full for a good week.

When you've got a coon treed or cornered it's kinda hard to tell if they're male or female. When ya knock 'em outta the tree with a nice head shot and they hit the ground DOA, you may have a treat. When you flip over the bandit and it's a male, you got the makin's of a toothpick. Cut that pecker bone off and hang it from a wire in the sun for around two weeks until it's all dried out. Take 'er down and sand it off. Then, when you got it all slicked up and beautified, go over to the grinder and put a 60% angle on the small end. Be sure to swish it around in the cleaning bucket of gas ... gotta make sure it's sanitized.

I was over in England years ago and went into a pub to see what all the ruckus was about in these establishments. The English are great bullshitters and love to talk politics. Also, the very first thing they'll tell an outsider is to never say anything bad about the Queen. A few of us got into a lively conversation, and they seemed to think I was all right so they bought me a beer. This one older gentleman seemed to be well versed in all subjects so I said, "Here, it's a present from the good ole US of A."

"What is it?"

"It's a toothpick that all us rednecks use."

They all looked at this new-fangled dental instrument in wonderment. He then asked, "Is it clean?"

"Sure is. Try 'er out."

He stuck it in his mouth and started doin' some toothpickin'.

"This is really nice. What's it made out of, mate?"

"Well, 'mate', it's made out of coon pecker! You know, a raccoon's dicky-do."

They all stopped when he blew the toothpick out of his mouth and it shot across the floor. I went to retrieve the gift and came back to more giggles and hoots. He ended up keeping the gift. To take it a step further with this coon pecker. Just drill a small hole in the side of this toothpick of a bone and you could get it to whistle. The one I gave this gentleman didn't have that added attraction. We call this a whistle dick.

My Uncle Red and Aunt Ida lived in the Risco school district. They could throw a rock across the ditch and hit Tallapoosa. You gotta remember, Tally was a population of around sixty folks. My three cousins Tommy, Jerri, and Judy were always up to something. They had ten years on my brother and I, but my Aunt Ida could really cook a coon and when she called to let us know coon was on the table, we didn't hesitate.

One thing about eatin' coon is that some people like it and some don't. I've known coon hunters that wouldn't eat coon, but most do. In the state of Missouri, if you kill a coon and sell its carcass you have to leave a back paw on. If you don't it might be mistaken for a pussycat. In other words, you want to know that you're not eatin' cat.

When cooking for eight to ten people, you must have at least two coons. Here's what you do when preparing coon: Wash him off, then par boil him to get rid of the gamey taste. Add some salt, pepper, red pepper, crab boil, and bay leaves into the pot. Bring to a boil, then to a slow boil, then to a simmer for about an hour.

In the next ten minutes, peel about four medium sweet potatoes and a couple of onions—these go around the coon. Next, put some onions and celery on the bottom of a roasting pan. After he's par boiled, drag the sucker out and put him in the roasting pan. Cut the sweet potatoes into quarters and fill in around the coon.

Here's what makes coon real tasty: fill up the pan a third of the way with milk so you can make a baste from the drippings. Stick it in the oven at 400 degrees. Make sure to baste every twenty minutes. You can drink a beer every twenty minutes then baste again. Repeat until coon is done.

In about an hour and a half, or whenever the meat is tender, start eatin'. It usually takes five beers on a young coon and six on the old one. Some folks put beer in with the coon to cook, but this is a waste of beer, so do not do this. The trimmings for eating coon or any other dinner generally include brown beans. I always felt Aunt Ida made the best. Cornbread can also be put on the table to soak up some of the juice and the bean gravy. Coon, brown beans, sweet potatoes, and collard greens, doesn't get any better. And, don't forget to remove the back paw before par boiling.

Coon Huntin' and Coon Cookin'

Our favorite ride... A '46' Willys.

Third Time's a Charm

My brother Eric could normally avoid trouble, for the most part. He could smell a bad fish or a shady situation coming from a mile away. I was always on the edge of trouble and schoolwork was a real chore. Folks would say under their breath, "What's wrong with that boy?" But, when my little brother Eric did get into trouble, he absolutely went the distance. At age fifteen he basically pissed off the state of Missouri. It was only for a short timeframe that this feat occurred; matter of fact it was done in less than five months. And the ending, of course, was not too good.

Strike One

Growing up on a farm meant we started driving earlier than most folks. We pulled cotton and soybean trailers around with tractors when we were thirteen years old. At fourteen, we disc and cultivated the fields and also drove the truck just about anywhere the truck could be driven on the farm or down a gravel road— those were the truck boundaries. Then at fifteen we drove on the blacktop. Most boys and some girls our age did this in farming communities and it was no big deal. Everyone knew to just stay out of our way.

It was late August and Eric had just gotten his Missouri driver's permit. He was a great driver—he was always on a tractor or liked backing up the truck to hook up to a trailer. He could drive anything with an engine and he liked a challenge. His mindset was, "Let's get the job done right, no need to go back over it twice."

New Madrid County was one big soybean field, and every year they had the Soybean Festival in Portageville just nine miles to the east of our house. This festival included a parade, carnival, fireworks, corndogs, and every once in a while, a fight or two. All good stuff.

We'd started to sell soybeans on the side for the past two years, so Dad was slowly spreading his wings.

We had a farmer down in Arkansas who called in and said he wanted to get a price on Dyer soybeans. Not too many people had them. We had grown some foundation seed for the University of Missouri in small plots, and we also had certified seed so we were on the right path. To cut to the chase, the farmer said he would be up to get 500 bushels of Dyer soybeans.

The banks like to know if you have your farming necessities in order before you ask for a big chunk of the loan to carry you through the winter…believe it, farming is one tough business. Soybeans back then, as they are now, were classified by variety. For example, Hood, Hill, Lee, Dare, Dyer, Pickett, Grant, Stewart and a whole bunch more were named after Civil War generals. Now they use mainly numbers.

This guy came up from around Marmaduke, kinda between Jonesboro and Paragould, up in that northeast corner of Arkansas. They were down-home folks but it was real pig country out there; people could barely talk or talk a lotta shit. So this Arkansas guy picked up his seed and headed back down south. He gave Dad a check, and two days later it bounced like a basketball. Dad called him and told him to send one that was legit. He said it was no problem.

No problem became a problem two weeks later when nothing was delivered. Dad was agitated, but he was also pretty good at taking things into his own hands to collect. It was late August; the mosquitos weren't even movin' it was so hot and muggy. Dad chose to drive down to Arkansas and confront this guy head on. Eric was told that he would be driving, which didn't seem to bother Eric. In fact, he was a little excited since he had just gotten his driver's permit and was going across the state line.

Dad and Eric headed out around 9:00 am and found this man's place out in the woolly's. Some country folk are generally a little skittish, it takes a while before they might warm up to your humor but this was the kind of a place where you could shoot someone and they might not ever show up again. Eric told me that everything looked good because the guy's pick-up was out front, so I guess they had him somewhat cornered.

Farmers sometimes had cash, but usually they didn't. But there was equipment and other loose ends that could be bartered with to bring things up to snuff. Our father had another weapon, and it was called 'Old Charter.' This was Kentucky straight bourbon that would be the equalizer and set the tone for this meeting.

Dad told Eric, "When I go through the front door, I want you to start hooking up those three rice buggies over in the back corner. Pull 'em right up front where we are now, at this very spot." Dad walked up to the door with the fifth of hooch. The farmer opened the door and Dad walked in to do business.

Eric was damn good at hookin' up trailers. One was easy, two maybe, but three was testing both his patience and skill level. He turned around and drove back to the rice buggies, and had to put his brain in gear to try and decipher this chore. A rice buggy was not small—it was a trailer that was tall with a slanted bed that pushed seed to fall to one side when unloading. Open the chute and there she goes. The wheels alone on one of these trailers was bigger than a drag car, and it looked like a Tonka toy. It also had an auger on the backside to pull grain up if it needed to go to a different elevation. It was just a hell of a set-up.

Eric decided to pull all three trailers out and kinda line 'em up with the hope that he could get lucky and get the tongue close enough to the hitch so he could put the pin into the lined up hole. Eric had the faith and the hope, but the love was not always there during this ordeal. After an hour of a lot of cussing and maneuvering around, he had all three rice buggies in line and hooked up to the pick-up.

He was ready to go, and looked around but Dad was nowhere in sight. It took Eric over an hour to hook these suckers up, but Dad must have been in a hell of a battle on the negotiating end. Dad had been inside for two and a half hours before he finally stumbled out the door at 1pm and made it into the passenger's seat. More than a little soused, he told Eric that he'd done a real good job at getting the buggies hooked up.

"When you pull out, be sure to make a big wide turn. Let's not hit any of those tires on a culvert."

Eric could do this part. He manufactured a way onto the gravel road without cutting any tires and two miles later he hit pavement. Dad also told him to take the back roads home. He showed him a real nice diamond ring that was marked up to the truth serum of Old Charter. Must have been some heavy negotiating.

Dad was lights out before they got to the pavement, just all crumpled up against the side of the truck, leaving Eric to navigate the road. When you're pulling one trailer, it will weave if something is not aligned. Pulling two trailers is hell, and I have no clue how my little brother made it back home with three, but he did have a pause in this very unorthodox task.

He was going maybe 30 MPH and made it back over to the Missouri side. He was within striking distance of home turf and, knowing Eric, he probably had a shit-eatin' grin on his face because he knew he was going to pull this off. Just six miles from the house, he passed Frailey. Then out of the clear blue, a smokey arrived on the scene. Yep, Missouri's finest met him head on, then slammed on the brakes and spun his machine around.

Eric saw the pretty blue lights come on and pulled 'er over, half on the shoulder and half on the road. Back then the police didn't park sideways to the rear of the vehicle, they just pulled in behind you and got out. They let the bravado of the uniform and sunglasses take over. The officer gave him a look like "What the hell is goin' on, boy? What is the problem?"

There was no problem here, Eric was just pulling three trailers down the road. Just three. To add to this jumbled-up equation there were no license plates on these trailers. Yes sir this was a humdinger of a situation. The officer walked to the front of the truck then back to where Eric had the truck window pulled down. I'm sure he was stepping it off from the back trailer to the front bumper of the truck to see how many feet he had on the road, not counting the sixteen tires that were on the pavement as well.

The officer leaned over and looked at Dad all balled up in the fetal position on the other side of the truck. He must have looked like he was part of the door.

The officer said, "License please."

Eric already had the driver's permit out and in his hand in less than two seconds. The officer looked at it and said, "This is a driver's permit."

Eric said, probably in a not-so-proud voice, "Yes sir."

The officer bent down some, his eyes looked to the passenger's side of the cab. "Is that your father over there?"

"Yes sir."

"Well, Eric, do you think you could find some way to get his driver's license out of his wallet?"

"Oh, yes sir." Eric said he had one hell of a time trying to move Dad into position to remove or better yet unharness his belt and pants to remove the wallet. But, once again Eric was successful. He looked through the wallet and found a semi-disintegrated card that said "Missouri Driver's License." After all this juggling with Dad's body for two minutes he handed the card to the officer.

The officer looked back at the trailers and said, "Where did you come from with these trailers?"

"Marmaduke, Arkansas, sir."

"You came that far with this monstrosity and didn't get pulled over?"

"No sir."

"Well, let me tell you Eric, first of all it's illegal to pull a train down a highway."

Eric's brain was now starting to malfunction as he thought, *holy shit*. The officer was drum beating on the top of the cab with his fingers studying him.

"This is what I'm goina do. I'm goina write both you and your father up on this one. How far do you live from here?"

"Six miles sir."

"I'll say this young man, I would normally haul your asses in, but I've never seen anybody in my whole life driving a mess like this down a highway. You go on your way and I'll let this part go. Make sure you give your father both those tickets tomorrow morning. I'm sure he's not goina be seein' too much tonight."

Yep, Eric hit a hard single to left but he was picked off of first. What's wrong with that boy?

Strike Two

One month later, in late September, you could tell the fall was coming because it had started to cool down. To make it even better there were very few mosquitos on the prowl. On this particular day, it was cool and the air was crisp with the smell of cotton gins burning off waste, which was just a great smell. Mom had her shift at the hospital and she got home at 4:00. An hour later she had just started to make supper. Dad was running around on the farm, I was in the family room watching TV, and Eric was scurrying around the house.

Mom saw Eric goin' here and there and said, "Eric, I need you to go up and get a paper at the IGA," (which was in Gideon). "The Post-Dispatch didn't come this morning and you know your father likes to check up on things. By the time you get back supper should almost be ready."

Eric rolled his eyes, "Yes maim, be right back."

I snickered and he flipped me off as he went out the door. The way I figured it, the trip should have taken under twenty minutes for a quick run into town. After about half an hour, though, Eric still wasn't back. We didn't have cell phones back then so communication fell under the SOL category, but not quite Pony Express.

Finally, I heard the car pull up to the side entrance rather than the car port. Eric came through the side door and immediately let Mom and the whole world know, "I've brought someone home."

Mom said to bring 'em in for supper.

I was right by the door all stretched out in Dad's Lazy Boy recliner enjoyin' life. Eric said to the person who was waiting at the bottom of the steps to "Come on in, sir." When he said "sir" I thought, *what the hell?* This man came through the door and I thought, *holy shit, Eric just brought home a real life state rod*!

The state trooper was dressed to the hilt. His pants had great creases, his shirt and tie were ever so sharp, his gun and belt rode up high on his hip, and he had that big smoky hat tucked under his left arm this was beyond far out. This guy also had epaulets with a gold bar on top to boot. Yep, he be a big dog.

Mom had her head down at the sink and Eric said, "Come on in, officer."

The word "officer" got Mom's attention, and as she turned around Eric said, "Mom, this is officer…" Eric paused (cat got your tongue little brother?) to look at the guy's nametag but the officer beat Eric to the draw.

"Officer Duckworth," he said.

Wow, Duckworth was standing right in our kitchen. This guy was a legend in the halls of Gideon high school. This was the trooper who nailed anybody and everybody.

Mom cut to the chase and said, "Well what do we have going on, Officer Duckworth?" in a nice tone.

"I pulled Eric over for having an expired license plate, Mrs. Littell."

Mom said, "I've been meaning to get that taken care of. We'll go do it this coming Monday."

Officer Duckworth said, "I don't doubt that, Mrs. Littell, but the other issue is that Eric carries a Driver's permit and there was no adult supervision in the passenger's seat." He turned to Eric and said, "Eric, I'm going to give you a ticket for driving without a license."

Mom said, "I understand, Officer Duckworth. You can sit down here at the table."

My brain said, *really?* But she was serious.

"Well, thank you, Mrs. Littell."

As my brain kicked into overdrive, I wanted to say, *Hey Mom, Why don't you just ask Officer Duckworth to stay for supper and tell him that Eric's going to say the blessing?*

In the meantime, I was turned around backwards with my knees dug into the bottom cushion of Dad's chair and my elbows burrowed into the padded top so I could have a front row seat. Hell, all I needed were some glasses and you would have thought I was watching this whole thing go down in 3D. Eric turned around as I started snickering under my breath, and he flipped me off.

Well, I can tell you this, Officer Duckworth was not only proficient but efficient as well; he knocked out that ticket in less than three minutes. What a guy. Officer Duckworth finished up and stood. He turned to Mom and said, "Mrs. Littell, be sure to get those license plates registered." Then he gave a half turn to little brother and said, "Eric, you need to make sure that when you have a Driver's Permit that an adult is in that passenger's seat … right, Mrs. Littell?"

My mom dropped a "yes sir." I think she was caught off guard. *Nice touch Officer Duckworth*, I thought as I saluted him from behind. Dad hadn't made it home yet but you could guarantee that the talk around the supper table that night was going to be taken up a notch.

With no meds in the sixties, my ADD mind would go into this quasi-moto-baseball-trance mode. I'd start recounting baseball games in my mind.

Yes folks, we're in the bottom of the ninth. The opposing Huckleberry team is up 1 to 0 with two outs. Our home team the Dingleberries have runners on second and third. Eric Littell is at the plate with a 1 and 2 count. Woodchuck Chukka winds and brings it home. Littell loads, swings, the ball is hit off the end of the bat, it's a "dying quail" folks as it's just over "Little Sparrow's" head, the Sioux Indian and second baseman as he drop steps and is going all out. But wait, it's "Fly with Eagles" the Blackfoot Indian centerfielder who has bolted hard to his left, and, and, oh my, here comes Chickasaw Duckworth, the right fielder. Duckworth has just come out of nowhere, as he kicks it into overdrive. Oh my gosh, they're all converging, it's going to be ugly folks as all three fielders go up into the air to see if one of them can snag this ball. Ladies and gentlemen, who will win this game?

And, oh look, Woodchuck Chukka is doing his famous "catch the ball dance" as he's circling the mound with the high step, head down format, minus the peyote. Fans, all I can tell you is that this ball has some hang time. The runner from second has now made the turn at third, he's heading home … it's the go ahead run.

But, back on the field Chickasaw Duckworth is coming in hard as he looks like a low-flying, green-head mallard that has just spotted a new cornfield. Chickasaw reaches out and, I don't see a ball on the field, but who's got the ball, where is the ball? Both Fly with Eagles and Little Sparrow are down and out from what was a massive collision but look it's Chickasaw Duckworth coming out of his barrel roll. Chickasaw is jumping up and down as he raises the glove above his head then brings his trusty piece of leather down to his chest. He reaches into the pocket as the ball is removed to let the Dingleberries and Eric Littell know that he truly will have the last word. And this is Chicken Hawk Chicken Shit on All-Sports … KSOB.

I score it Duckworth 1, Littell 0

Third Strike ... NO SHIT

It was late October and had started to cool down. At supper on a Friday night Dad said he wanted Eric to drive him up to Caledonia to a funeral in the hills of Missouri. The hill country was where a lot of Mom's clan was from. My Mom was not feeling well so Dad would be the stand-in guy at the funeral. Dad said, "Mark, you're staying at the house with your mother in case she needs anything."

The Reiffers had a tendency to like the liquid stuff. It didn't matter what the occasion was, a wedding, funeral or a confirmation were all acts of celebration. It was all about eatin', drinkin', and family at these gatherings. By the end of any event some of my uncles, with aunts included, had probably thought they'd died and gone to hell and back.

When Eric was told he was doing the driving, he just rolled his eyes and believe me, I held my breath and didn't snicker because I did not want to be in the backseat. Yup, Eric was goina go see God-fearin' people at a funeral in the Bible Belt.

The funeral was at eleven on Saturday morning and it was going to take close to three hours to get up to this small town of a hundred-plus people in what many would call a village. Dad decided to take the back way up to Caledonia; it was around 135 miles of Missouri back roads. Some were paved of course, but you still had potholes that would knock everything out of alignment. You drove with both hands on the wheel.

Early the next morning, I heard through my muffled pillow Eric being told to take his tie and put the shoe brush onto those dusty-lookin' shoes. Mom still got up and made 'em a quick breakfast and sent them out the door. *Good luck and have fun little brother,* I thought.

I heard Eric crank up the '69 Grand Marquis that had a 390 barrel under the hood. Yes, it could and would haul ass. My father would always put a Bible on the dash when he went toward hill country in Missouri or any other state for that matter, so if he got stopped it just might ward off some of those evil spirits lurking in the woods.

As the story continues, Eric crossed the St. Francis River and passed just outside the city limits of Poplar Bluff from the east where it starts to get hilly. Eric and I drove this almost every day during the summer because we played baseball for Poplar Bluff American Legion for three years. They made it through the "Bluff" and were heading north toward Ironton. To give you a bearing, they were just on the outskirts of the Ozarks to the east but heading north. You didn't see much water but you still had a lot of up and down hills that would have half-mile stretches going down and half-mile stretches going up on a two-lane road. We called these passing lanes.

It really would hack you off if you were setting behind some old fart goin' 55 MPH when the speed limit on the back roads was 65 MPH. Our speed limit was generally 75 MPH in the hills but you had to watch out for that bad boy with the antlers; you don't want a deer lying across the front of your grill.

I guess Eric was sailing but this car in front of him was poking along at the crest of the hill. Eric backed it down and Dad said, "Put this thing into passing gear and get around this guy."

Eric had no problem with this so he floored it. Just before he hit the bottom of the hill, the passing gear kicked in; now he was flying by the guy on the upside of the hill and starting to pull back into his lane midway through the hill. He now saw a car coming just over the top of the hill so he maneuvered back into his lane. He felt pretty good about this nice tactical stance of getting around slow Joe. The only problem he had was that the car coming at him in the other lane was a smokey—yup, it was a full-fledged Missouri State Trooper with those big blue bubblegum lights.

Before Eric hit the top of the hill he could see in the rear view that the lights were real pretty. Eric said he let out his normal word of disgust when around Mom or Dad: crap. Dad's take was, "Just kick 'er back to 65 MPH and let him pull you over."

Believe me, it's hard to pull off in hill country because first off, it's a narrow two-lane road, and second, you have a ditch or a drop off on either side. There's just nowhere to go when you're up in this neck of woods. So it took Eric a while to find a gravel road that he could swing into and stop the truck.

As usual the officer was setting there for a while behind him just checkin' out his license plate to see that he wasn't a wanted criminal. He knew Eric was squirming but he waited a minute before he got out and proceeded to come toward the Marquis.

Dad told Eric, "Let me do the talking once he gets past your license."

Eric rolled his eyes as he rolled down the window. The officer said, "Your license please." Eric handed him the crumpled up driver's permit. I asked Eric if he had the dark sunglasses and the smokey hat. He said, "You bet." Badass.

He looked at the papers for ten seconds or so and he said, "This is a driver's permit."

Eric said, "Yes sir."

He said, "Do you know what you might have done wrong? Do you know why I pulled you over?"

Eric said, "Well, I was passing a car and getting back into my lane, sir."

Dad decided to chime in as he said, "I'm his father, officer. I wanted Eric to kick it into passing gear and get around that car. We're goin' to a funeral over here in the hills."

The officer leaned forward and said, "Well, Mr. Littell, let me say this. Eric did find passing gear…he found passing gear at 89 MPH going up the grade and that's just not going to fly out here in the hills."

Yes-sir-ee, Eric was guilty on the spot. Where I really think Eric screwed up was when he rolled the window down and instead of leaving the Bible on the dash, he should have been clutching it next to his heart. They went to the funeral and paid their respects to the family. After, Eric drove back home with his third ticket. I guess you might say he easily reached third base, no slide required. It was a stand up triple. *Littell takes a lead off of third but the third baseman walks three steps and tags him … oh no, the hidden ball trick!* Dumbass.

State Of Missouri vs. Eric Littell

After Eric's third run-in with the law, the law caught up with him. Yep, little brother received a summons in the mail in the middle of November that he was to appear at the New Madrid County Court House in

December. Dad said, "It's Juvenile Court, so we're going to go over and see what's going on then we'll just take it from there."

Yeah, Eric was on edge for the next three weeks and then the day came to go to court. For some reason Dad drove—what a brilliant idea. Yes, Eric was a little pale and sickly as they left the house that day. Driving over to New Madrid was around a twenty-mile jaunt. For that twenty-mile stretch, nobody stopped them or, better yet, no tickets were issued and they made it to the county seat unscathed. They walked up the steps and through the doors of the courthouse and didn't have to look long before they spotted the sign that said, "Eric you are in trouble"... I mean "Juvenile Court."

They walked in and noticed that nobody was in there except this kinda hefty lookin' guy behind the desk looking down at some papers. He said, "Take a seat, I'll be with you in a minute."

They sat down and were quiet because there wasn't much to say, though I think Eric was wondering where all the criminals were. He said his mind was racing. Yep, all that was in this squared-off room with a twelve-foot ceiling was Eric, Dad, Boss Hog, and GOD.

The man at the desk looked up and said, "I'm Jimmy Joe Bloomfield, I'm the juvenile officer and you must be Eric Littell."

Eric said, *"I'm the bad ass"* in his mind but "Yes sir" came out crystal clear.

"Are you Eric's father?"

"Yes sir, I'm Alan Littell, sir."

"Mr. Littell, you can stay seated, but Eric, you need to come forward and stand up here in front of the desk." Eric moved to stand in front of the desk and the big guy looked down on him. "Well Eric … you have had a very interesting life in the past four months. How did you do it? This is quite an accomplishment." Officer Bloomfield looked down at the paperwork in his open file and said, "Whew boy, three infractions in a four-month period … that's hard to top. Eric, let me ask you a question. Are you guilty of all these infractions?

A pause, "Oh yes, sir?"

"And, I see your Daddy here has paid the fines."

"Yes sir."

"Well, it seems that paying fines isn't going to get your attention and probably takin' your Driver's permit away until you turn sixteen will not keep you from behind the wheel. Eric, you stay right there, I got something that might start to bring you around to some awareness." He walked through another door and came back into the room carrying something. He sat down and with both hands picked up a large book and slapped it down right in front of Eric. "Eric, what does this say?"

"Missouri Driver's Manual."

"Well, Eric, I want you to write out this manual in free hand. You can use either your pen or pencil and have this back over to me, let's say January 12th. Be here at 10:00am. You write this with your own hand front cover to back cover and I will let you get your Missouri Driver's license in February. Your hand only, do you understand Eric?"

"Yes sir."

"Mr. Littell," he added as Dad stood. "You are going to have to keep a better watch on this boy here … do you understand?"

"Yes sir."

While walking out of the room of hell, Eric took knee-buckling paces down the creaking stairs. Not a word was said until they had cleared the steps of the courthouse. Dad stopped and turned to Eric and said, "Hell, I knew they were going to throw the book at you but I didn't know they'd make you write the damn thing."

Eric wasn't laughing. An ice cream cone at the local Dairy Queen couldn't even put a smile on Eric's face, but he did endure. When Eric got back he was pissed off that he was going to have to write out this whole damn thing about a bunch of highway shit. Yes, he wrote over Christmas vacation but he did have a plan to put some of his buddies to work; he told 'em to just do some chicken scratching like he was doing, but that buddy system part didn't last long. Eric went back over in January and Officer Bloomfield approved his work. He also asked Eric if his hand had gotten tired.

"Oh you bet, yes sir that got my attention."

"Yeah boy, you'll ace that written test for sure."

The Way Eric And I See It ...

Mom and Dad should have been writing the manual. Dad told Eric to drive the back roads pullin' a train. Mom told Eric to go into town and get the newspaper. And Dad said to floor it. But, the Bible says, "Honor thy father and mother."

Eric's Numbers To Date ...

Eric has been in sales with two companies for forty years. He will put on between 40,000 to 50,000 miles a year, and every day he gets better at avoiding the almighty state trooper and the long reach of the law. I asked Eric once, "How many tickets do you get a year?"

In his estimation, he would get a ticket a year. In my calculation he has been written up forty times with an average ticket costing, let's say $100. Yes, that's $4,000. That's a year of school in a Junior College. Mom and Dad always told us that getting an education pays.

Loco Weed

The Bootheel was once a swamp and every now and then it would remind us that if the flora was not maintained for, say, five years or so, it could quickly turn into a jungle. To even get to the other side of our ditches you would have to maneuver down this massive cut that pushed water to the Mississippi River. But first and foremost, you had to look out for water moccasins. Hell, there could be anywhere from ten to twenty of these nasty, foul-smellin' snakes all balled up and tucked away keepin' warm. All these suckers do is breed and make more little snakes. Folks out West talk about how bad a rattlesnake can be, well, at least the rattlesnake gives you some warning, whereas that water moccasin is already on top of you. If you're close that attack mode is triggered. Can you only imagine a tennis shoe falling into that nice little safe haven of baby moccasins? It's their home turf, it's their comfort zone…then it's your foot.

Second, to cut across you have to have the ability to map out and maneuver around any water obstacle that would present itself at the bottom of the ditch. Very rarely would a ditch be dry. Third, when you got to the other side you then had to crawl and duck around sassafras and red-topped "shoemake" bushes to go up and out. Then there were always these huge weeds with a funny looking leaf, ten, maybe twelve feet high. There were tons of 'em growing all over the place.

Every five years, the Army Corps of Engineers would dragline and clean out the ditches to maintain the flow of water. Heavy rains brought in silt and all kinds of crap. Yes, the Bootheel does get a bit of water, with some big flooding and an occasional tornado as added attractions. To do the cleaning of these ditches right and be fair to each farmer, the Corp of Engineers would, during one five-year stretch, clean out the Fletcher side; then, five years later, they would clean out the Littell side. The Corps would dump all this silt and debris on your land and then it was your responsibility as a landowner to bulldoze this back into your acreage. It was just an abundant amount of waste that created these great mounds to play on and have war games.

I enjoyed setting down and watching the dragline with that big bucket make a long swipe to the other side. It would just drag, lift, and then dump. I liked getting close to where the operator was going to dump— it made a slushy sound when the door of the bucket would open and this sludgy deposit would fall and hit the ground. Half of my body would get splattered and the driver would laugh. It was fun.

Yes siree, we lived 200 yards off of No. 5 ditch and had all kinds of amusing things to explore. When I was ten, my Dad was standing out in front of the house watching this colossal truck with a huge water tank on board. It also carried this humongous spray gun that was mounted to this swivel seat that looked like it came off of a US Naval destroyer. All this was placed in the middle of the bed. This truck was lined up and hugging the top of the ditch. It was just pokin' along real slow on our side of the ditch, shooting out a stream of yellow liquid from the big ole spray gun. It looked like piss, and what a blast it was at the end of the nozzle. It shot outta there sixty or seventy feet, maybe further.

Since I was always extremely curious at this time of my life, or any other time for that matter, I decided to stand next to Dad and get his take on what was going on. Dad was just standing there with his arms folded taking a drag off his camel when needed. I didn't say anything for a minute or so, as I tried to absorb what kind of scenario we had goin' on here. This particular stretch of the farm was a quarter mile long, so it took 'em over fifteen minutes to get to the end of our farm before they crossed over and started on the next farm.

One thing that puzzled me was this guy running the spray gun. He had a white suit on from top to bottom and a mask as well. I knew he had to have been smoking in this get-up—it was May and it must have been 80 degrees. Aliens? Nope, it was the "Feds"—you know, the EPA.

My question to my Dad was, "What's goin' on with that big truck out there?"

"Well, son, they're sprayin' for loco weed. That's those tall weeds you and Eric hang onto when you're goin' up and down the ditch."

"What's loco weed?"

"Well, it makes cows sick … makes 'em go crazy."

"Dad, we haven't got any cows." It was true. The closest cow to us was fifty miles away in either direction.

He turned his head and said, "Well, it makes people sick too."

"Do people eat it?"

"Mark, I really can't say, but don't you go eatin' it. Don't go grinding it up, I know you and Eric get these ideas. And most definitely don't try smoking it either. It'll make you go crazy. You do hear me loud and clear on this?"

A big "Yes sir" came right back as I made eye contact with Dad. Dad always said, "If you're shakin' hands with a guy and there's no eye contact, DON'T TRUST HIM."

Dad cured me of ever wanting a cigarette at age five when we were over at Grandpa Reiffer's house one Saturday night. Back then, the women would sit in one room and the men in another. In this case, the ladies were in the dining room and the men in the living room. My brother and I always hung out with the guys, as we both got tired of the aunts and grandma smooching us and the lipstick that came with it. In the living room there was always a bunch of boring and uninteresting chatter. In other words they were talking a lot of shit that Eric and I didn't understand or particularly care about. Eric was bouncing up and down on my grandpa's boot, while grandpa crossed one knee over the other and sat back and smoked his pipe, multi-tasking.

My mind was on wanting to smoke my dad's Camel cigarette. I just kept buggin' the shit out of him to let me suck on that cigarette. Well, finally he had had enough. He looked across the room at my grandpa and said, "Bill, I'm goina cure this boy right now of ever wanting to smoke."

Grandpa said, "Good a time as any."

Dad said, "Mark?"

"Yes sir."

"Take a sip off this cigarette just like you're drinkin' a soda. Now suck in hard."

"All right." I went for it, just like a newborn calf lookin' for mama's tit. "Now suck hard," and I did—yeah, I really did turn green and coughed up a storm that would never end. Holy shit.

All the men were just howlin' up a storm. Mother bear heard her cub in distress and yelled out, "What's wrong with Mark?" Not only did Dad catch hell, but every human being with a penis in that room thought the wrath of God had seeped in through the walls.

No, I never touched a cigarette again. But when I got to around ten years old, the new thing was to smoke wild grape vines. These tasted like pure bat shit. I tried two or three, and one of my buddies said to inhale it and not suck and puff it. It didn't take me long to figure out this was a bunch of shit. Just like with the cigarette, I was forever cured of wanting to smoke. But what business mind I had took over for a split second. Maybe I could corner the market with "Wild Grape Vine Smokes." Product credibility would come from the old Chinese mantra, "It good for you." My slogan would be, "Tastes like Panther Piss but heals and cures anything and everything." So much for the cerebral thought. I moved on when I realized distribution was going to be a tough road to hoe.

But, there is an ironic side to this story. When Eric and I were twelve or so, one of the really fun things Dad wanted us to do was burn things. We had this red cub cadet tractor we used to mess around on. We also had the perfect size trailer for this little fart of a machine. When on a burn mission, we had a thirty-gallon propane tank in this trailer, and attached to the tank was a twenty-five-foot hose that had a seven-foot torch as the main feature. Yes, it would throw out a flame and in our assessment, it was a "f'ing flame thrower."

My dad liked a clean farm, so we would burn fencerows, wheat fields, and of course, ditches where this loco weed was more than plentiful. After doing this chore, we were always ever so quiet at the dinner table. For some odd reason, Mom would always ask Dad, "What's wrong with the boys? They're awfully quiet and peaceful, didn't even eat as much."

Dad said, "They're just tired."

Are you shitin' me? (a common baseball term). We were STONED and didn't know it! Although Eric and I never smoked a joint, I can truthfully say during our teen years we were enlightened many times by default.

In the fifties and sixties I guess a lot of people knew about marijuana, and that's what those big weeds were on the ditch that grew up so tall. But for us they were just excellent cover to hide in while playing war and occasionally they were fun to burn. Right now, you can buy this loco weed anywhere—the shit is even legal in a few states and all you have to do is tell some flunky-ass doctor that you have a stress disorder or a sore that needs healed up and they'll issue you a card to get loco weed just about anywhere. And it's good for life. I'm sure this is one way of keeping that robust economy on the go. Go get that prescription, but first try out "Wild Grape Vine Smokes." It's good for you.

Sunday Rat Killin'

My family were churchgoers—we went to the First United Methodist Church. Living in the Bible Belt was a big chore for most young folks, especially when you came from a small town. You were put under the microscope, plus there was a lot of competition in towns of this size because everyone knew what you wore, when you got it, and how much it cost. You might say it wasn't a real Christian way of lookin' at things, even though there were six to seven churches in the area.

The First Baptist Church was the big one in the community, then you had the Pentecost which was big as well. The Baptist could sing but the Pentecost could raise the roof and shake the floor... Hallelujah! The Catholics had to drive to Malden, which was around ten miles to the north. We had two families in Gideon that made this trip every Sunday. Dr. Alan Gubin was our doctor and he was Jewish, so I've been to some bar mitzvahs in my life. This covers most of the bases of religion in Gideon. For the most part we all hung out together, but us Methodists were considered heathens. In our church basement we had dances and to top it off we had a pool table. Those Methodist are just playin' with the Devil ... 8 ball to the corner pocket.

On the other side of the coin, Gideon had no fewer than four to five bars, and some that were floaters—

El Morraco back in the day

146

the kind that would be here today and gone tomorrow. There was Murphy's Pool Hall that was across the street from the Gideon Anderson lumber company, and Gibbs bar which was right smack dab in the center of town and had a real pretty round window that was blue. The Idle Hour Club wasn't always idle—on certain nights it was hoppin'. Then, there was the El Morocco which was just over the train tracks on the north side and was the wildest place around. If you were a goer of the El Morocco you were for sure goin' to Hell. A few people of this era carried a pistol close, either on 'em or in the truck. You might have only one to two "killin's" a year, but alcohol and weapons didn't mix, and apparently neither did some of the women.

My mom filled me in on the weapons of choice. She was an RN and saw a lot of people come into the hospital with both gunshot and knife wounds. Some walked out, some didn't. Doctors McCoy, McKaskle, and Gubin were always on call.

After church we would go back home to eat Sunday dinner. Dinner was lunch to us and supper was dinner to farm families. If we were livin' high on the hog we might go over to Clarkton and eat at the Clarktonian Café—a three-mile trip for a real tasty meal. The Clarktonian was hooked onto a gas station on the south end of town and was known for its roast beef and mashed potatoes. The cost was $2.75, and with a drink it was $3.00 …

expensive but manageable. If you wanted to splurge you went to the Anderson House Hotel in Gideon. They had around four rooms that were rented out, but mainly it was kept open for Mr. and Mrs. Anderson when they came down from St. Louis. They owned the Gideon Anderson Lumber Company, which was the lifeblood of Gideon for years. When you ate at the Anderson House it was considered high cotton. They were known for their fried chicken, which was served family style, meaning all the trimmings were served in big bowls. Mashed potatoes, green beans, corn, baked rolls and cornbread would just keep comin' as long as you could shovel it in your mouth. The cost was $4.25 and this included the drink, but dessert was $.75 extra. It was worth it but it did stretch the pocketbook.

After a Sunday dinner there would usually be a short pause or a break. Once everybody got a second wind, my mom and dad would sometimes take a drive to check out the farm and in all probability take a break from my brother and me, the Gruesome Twosome.

It was a cool March day in the Bootheel. My dad did not like having rats around and he told Eric and me that we could have free rein on getting rid of the rat population. We were ages fourteen and thirteen and were going to make a mark on the agriculture community as rat exterminators. This would be a big mistake on Dad's part, but it ended up being worse on me and Eric.

We put our brains to work and agreed that two heads were better than one. To exterminate these critters we decided to use diesel, gas, and Fritz.

This was the experimental stage of our lives, so for two weekends on Sunday afternoons we took care of and killed all the rats over at the grain bins across the road. Our method was simple: we took five gallons of gas and five gallons of diesel, then poured them down the hole and waited for the rats to come out. Farm gas only cost about $0.28 a gallon and diesel was even less, so for about $2.50 you could literally have a blast. When a lot of rats would come out, that's when it got fun. Each of us carried a baseball bat or a machete, and when these suckers came out drenched in this concoction of gas and diesel, they would scurry around in circles, blinded. We'd beat the shit out of 'em or chop 'em up with the machete. Fritz got in the action too. He'd grab one and flip it up in the air or put it back into play where Eric and I could get back in the action. What a dog, he could really hunt!

On one particular Sunday, we were getting all the goodies together to go out to do some rat killin' when Eric said, "Let's go to the grain bins."

I said "No, I think we got all the rats over there."

"Where do we go then?"

I paused and thought. "That's easy, the pump house."

The pump house was a small building, eight by ten feet. This was where our main water source was for the house. We put down a point well sixteen feet for our water supply, then built the house around the well. We heavily insulated the walls so it wouldn't freeze, and added a small door and a light that was always kept on to keep the chill out. Our pump house was right behind the garage, forty feet from the back door. Rather than having a long run, this would help keep the pipes from freezing and everybody would be happy.

Hum baby, were goina have a real good time; new huntin' territory and I was sure there were rats galore under the pump house. We dumped in five gallons of gas and five gallons of diesel down the holes. Fritz was in his ready position. Mom and Dad had just left for their Sunday drive. We really wanted to do a good job on this one since it was right next to the house. We didn't really tell our folks about the ten gallons of gas and diesel, or about the two previous excursions over at the grain bins. We had a 500-gallon diesel tank and a 1000-gallon gas tank—once again, this stuff was cheap. So, for less than $3.00 we were goina have a blast. Well, sorta.

We were waiting for some action to happen, but nothing was falling our way. I told Eric, "I'm goina go inside the pump house and see if they might have come out on the inside."

The pump house light was on and I saw the rat holes. They were about the size of the calf on your leg. Some of these rats got pretty big so you definitely didn't want to get bit by one of these suckers. I could see why people ate these things in third world countries.

Hallelujah, I saw a rat stick his head up. He saw me and exited to the outside. I yelled out to Eric that a rat was comin' out. "Go git 'em!" But my voice was muffled from all the insulation.

Eric and Fritz were on the outside doing their thing and I waited for probably close to a minute to see if anything might come back my way. Finally, one fat sucker came scurrying back into the pump house through the door, and holy moly he was on fire! Literally. Flames were flickering on his hairy back and before I could stop him, he was scampering back down into the hole.

"Holy shit!"

Before I got the "-it out of my mouth, there was an explosion that blew me right out the door. Smoke trailed me right outside where I was on the grass holding my ears, my head ringing. Worse, my brother was rollin' in the grass laughin' his ass off. Brotherly love took over and I proceed to pound him. Fritz decided to join in as he thought this was fun time.

What had happened was my brother had decided to take out his matchbook. He started flipping matches at this fat rat that was drenched in this gas-diesel concoction. Well, he got lucky, and it caught the vermin on fire. The rat hit the side of the pump house running and fell down the hole we'd filled with gas-diesel. KA-BLEW-EE!!! I didn't have a chance.

My head got better as I got Eric on the ground and started swatting at him. The blast was over in seconds and the pump house was now on fire, quickly ruining our fun. Smoke was comin' out from underneath and on the west side where the rat went in for a kamikaze. The smoke was white at first, then it turned black.

My ass was grass at this point. Eric always got a free ride. We high-tailed it to the shop to get shovels and pick-axes and we turned the water hose on from the garden. Another great idea. Now we started putting holes in the side of the pump house. We were getting smarter, and decided we'd put dirt down the holes and put the fire out this way, by smothering it. Eventually we got the fire out and then Mom and Dad returned. This was not one of my better moments of life. Even Fritz knew when to exit.

Aunt Bea

Not everybody can say this, but Brother Eric and I had a for-real Aunt Bea who had freckles, flaming red hair, wore glasses, and had just the prettiest gold tooth when she smiled. Aunt Bea was no kin to us but took over as our grandmother when she was in a car wreck out in Colorado with my grandparents. They didn't live long but Aunt Bea was thrown from the car and made it out alive and took charge.

She was a real corker and told us plenty of stories about those hard times in the thirties, forties, and fifties. She was married but we never met husband John who was twenty years her senior. They came up from El Dorado, Arkansas and bought the El Morocco lock, stock, and barrel in Gideon. That was the saloon on the north side of the tracks. For entertainment, believe me, they had it all. I've said it before and I'll say it again, if you're hangin out at the El Morocco there was a damn good chance you'd end up going to hell. They had all the booze you wanted, all kinds of card games goin' on, pool sharks just layin' low to go in for the kill, and there were a few women floatin' around that just might take you for a ride … in house of course. They also had the enforcers who carried a .38 special, a six shooter that was better known as a "Saturday Night Special." It was a safe bet that the St. Louis mob took their cut as well.

Aunt Bea would always talk about takin' trips down to Hot Springs, Arkansas where she and John went to relax with some of those nice folks from St. Louis. She used to say, "Honey, me and John never spent a dime on anything."

After takin' that fall harvest outta the field, some of those curious farmers and sharecroppers would sneak into the El Morocco not knowing that they would be walkin' into quicksand. There was a hell of a chance that they just might end up leavin' most of that hard-earned cash, or worse, the deed to their land at the door.

It was just hard times. If you didn't have a few chickens and a milk cow it would be tough, and food was scarce unless you shot it. That all mighty greenback was just not there. Hell, Aunt Bea had all kinds of cash hidden all over the house. Behind the oven the money was tucked away and kept warm, and sometimes it was wrapped up and stuck under the mattress. She slept like a baby. She even had it wrapped up in tin foil in the freezer ... this was what she called her cold cash.

But let me make this clear: Aunt Bea always gave back. She was a pillar of the community and also a board member of the Gideon United Methodist Church ... that's probably how we got the pool table. The Baptist and Pentecost folk never set foot in our church. Yep, we could dance and shoot pool in the basement and we were all goina go to hell, judgment had been passed.

Husband John was a businessman but he also liked to bird hunt. A class act bird dog is a pretty penny, and Aunt Bea was always talkin' about having to feed those mangy four-legged critters. Yeah, she thought they were just a real pain in the butt.

One day Aunt Bea was driving this new Oldsmobile '88 that John had bought her. It was maroon with a light tan interior, just real sharp, and she'd had it for about a month. She decided to get outta the house and go for a drive. She said to herself, "Well I'll just swing by the El Morocco."

She made the turn and saw John out front talkin' to a friend of his—both had one leg propped up on the back bumper of this so-called friend's truck. Aunt Bea didn't pay too much attention to it, but there was a dog in the back of the truck. So she started waving and puttin' on a big smile and hollered out, "Hey, Honey." He waved and this goody-two-shoes friend of his tipped his cap as Aunt Bea kept on polkin' along.

To cut to the chase, John came home a couple hours later and said, "Honey, I got a real good deal worked out but the deal involves with your car."

"Whataya mean, involves my car?"

"Well that buddy of mine you saw me talkin' to, and believe me, I whittled him down, said after you drove by, that, he'd trade his dog straight up for that 88 Olds Ms. Bea was drivin'. Bea, this is just one heck of a dog."

"Really? I suppose this dog shoots the bird, fetches the bird, cleans the bird, then cooks the bird?"

"Aww Bea, this is a real high-cotton dog. I'll be getting you another car real soon."

Aunt Bea's response was, "Not soon enough."

Well, he brought the dog home and put him out in the cage with the others. For the price he paid Aunt Bea thought he'd be sleepin' between them in bed. She waited two days and there was no car in the garage so she decided to go buy a milk cow. There was a guy over off of No. 3 ditch that had a couple and Aunt Bea asked if he'd sell one. She paid him and asked if he could walk it over and tie it to the telephone post in the side yard.

Well wouldn't you know it, John came walkin' in and had heard down at the saloon that there was a milk cow in their side yard. Aunt Bea wanted to clear him up on this. "No John, this is my milk cow in my side yard. You can go out and barter for a dog, well I can go out and buy a milk cow."

Two days later she had her new car. And what about that dog John traded for? Ended up bein' the worst dog of the bunch. Dog couldn't hunt a stuffed bird.

Aunt Bea

Field of Fluff

*E*arly on in the fifties when I was learning how to talk we called a black person "colored." A few years later that word would come to pass and the word "black" would hang around for a while, before the final change would land and "African American" would be used to define a race. When you went into most towns in the delta and the South you would, of course, pass by a few storefronts, a dive of a cafe or maybe a few shops that might have a sign stating "NO BLACKS" or "BLACK IN THE BACK." This small, sun-bleached sign would be tucked away in the lower corner of the window. It usually looked like it might disintegrate if it were to fall over, as if it had been there awhile.

This declaration of refusal was a warning: "Don't step out of line." Of course this view by a few of the local Christians was stated in a Bible verse. Somewhere I guess this Bible verse said that the Black, the Brown, the Yellow, and the Purple were not acceptable under certain circumstances. When I asked one of my buddies still livin' in the Boot if they had ever found that particular Bible passage he told me, "Nope, they're still having trouble locating that verse."

At the ripe age of seventeen, I had seen my fair share of both the good and not so good events of the world. But on this one particular day over summer break I would end up helping my Mom. She was the Head Start nurse over a six county area in the Bootheel—that's a lot of ground to cover. Dr. Gubin, who coordinated any medical matters, told Mom she was going to need some help with all these kids. "Ask Mark if he would like to make $25 to stick kids and draw blood out of their fingers."

I jumped at that offer. It sounded like fun, and $25 bucks in 1970 was a boatload. It was early when we left the house; I knew well that Mom always had to get her coffee so we stopped in this little café right off the main drag in Portageville. I walked in with Mom to this dingy dive of a place, with yellow walls that were once white. Mom said, "Mark, do you want something?"

"Chocolate milk," I said.

As I was looking through the opening where they shoved out the chow, my eyes zoomed into the kitchen where I saw the same size hole on the other wall. I saw some black men moving around talkin' to a lady through this now curious opening.

"Hey, Mom?"

"Yes, Mark."

"What's that on the other side of the wall? There's some black men back there movin' around…"

She put her finger to her mouth with the shush sign, then whispered, "I'll tell you outside."

We made it out the door and Mom said, "That's where the blacks eat."

I remember thinking, *Really, are you shitin' me* (a common baseball term) *this is 1970*! *That's a bunch of crap*. Yes, it was obvious it sent the wrong message. I knew in other parts of the country people were prejudice, but for some reason southern folk hung on a little longer. Hell, who was I kiddin' there was prejudice pretty much everywhere.

The way my brother and I were brought up was definitely different, but parenting was tough no matter what era. Am I guilty of racist thoughts or a slip of the tongue? Yes, I too am guilty and raise my hand. But my parents did their best to raise us right and treat people like people.

One of the reasons I believe my upbringing was different was because we were always around black workers, especially during cotton chopping. Cotton chopping occurred once a year in the spring. When someone chops cotton they are thinning out the excess cotton when it's around three or four inches tall. This gives the roots room to spread.

I remember well chopping cotton with no less than fifty blacks who had come out to work. They parked their two buses next to the field one early morning. The head man had agreed with my father on ten cents per row to chop cotton. The rows were a quarter mile long. My dad had told us the night before that my brother Eric and I were going to chop cotton for a half day. I was eight, and Eric was right behind me.

In the morning, we ate some breakfast and walked out the door at seven. Mom gave each one of us a quart jar of water with ice in it as we headed out. Sunscreen we didn't know about then, but we made sure we wore hats. We made a bee line to the tool shed where we rummaged through this mess of shovels, picks, axes, and augers—just all kinds of handles stickin' up. Dad stuck his head around the corner and said, "Boys, I already got your hoes leanin' up against the shop...let's go."

We picked up the pace as we left with a hoe in one hand and a quart jar of water resting on our forearm. It was only a couple hundred yards from the shed to where everyone was setting up to make a line. They put Eric and me at the end by this lady with a huge sunbonnet. She was going to show us what to chop and what to not chop. We caught on pretty fast.

Sometime after we started, they started singin' Gospel music with a nice beat. Elvis was runnin' late but yeah baby there was some rhythm in that cotton field. I hoed from the left side and Eric from the right, just like swingin' a bat. At the end row the same lady would touch up our hoe with a file to keep it sharp. Both of us were sweatin' like dogs but felt safe and cared for. The singin' was good so we had a beat goin' with the hoe— we were getting the job done.

The next year we chopped again but this was way different. These were folks from Old Mexico who went around in two buses doing the same thing—lookin' for work then choppin' up a storm. At lunch break they started a fire with some wood they had brought out of the back of the bus. After the fire was goin', they put down two cinder blocks on each side of the fire for this big disc blade to rest on ... this was their grill. They got the grill hot, buttered up the tortillas, then did a throw down on a polished disc blade. Yep, made sense to me.

Before they ate and before they started choppin', at the end row, they kept makin' this hand gesture in front of their body. I had seen this before. A couple of years later I would find out that they were making the sign of the cross. It was fun being around these folks. We couldn't understand a word they were saying but you could tell they liked to work. The phrase "time is money" now came into the thought process. They definitely got after it; they wanted to get finished so they could move on to another farmer and another field. Hell, why not when the going rate per row had gone up to twelve cents.

One year, dad had some black folks that came by and asked if they could pick the end rows of the cotton. Dad agreed and was happy about someone comin' by to do the job that a cotton picker (machine) would miss. They made some money and so did he. Eric and I would go out to join in and pick these short end rows alongside them. These rows dropped off where the cotton picker spindles couldn't reach. We'd be down on our knees pullin' either a seven-foot or nine-foot sack through the rows and stuffin' it with cotton. Yep, all my brain was sayin' was "pickin', pullin', and stuffin'."

At age eleven the one thing that got my attention more than anything, that would forever stick out so much in my thoughts, was when we were pickin' cotton with this group and a lady was giving birth right next to the cotton trailer. With all the commotion going on, Eric and I made a quick pass by the makeshift delivery area. It was around 10:30 in the morning, and we were both thinkin', "Hope this kid comes before lunch."

It was hard to swallow…you know all that screamin' and shit. All the pickers came in four cars that were parked close to the trailer next to this field of fluff. There was no room to go havin' a baby in a car, so a blanket was spread out on the ground just a little under the middle of the trailer. The bed was made and a pillow was placed under her head in the shade. I could tell the ladies caring for her knew how to go about delivering a baby. Mom was at the hospital workin' so these would be what they called midwives.

Eric and I traipsed over to the side of the trailer where the water bucket and scales were hangin' to get a closer look at the overall situation. We peeked over at the scene and saw a few folks helpin' out. Most of the people, though, were still in the field pickin' away. After our look-see, we dropped it into first gear as we both went into what you might call the "haul-ass mode." Like nothing ever happened, we went right back to pickin' cotton quickly. It made me want to start singin' but nobody else was singin', and I didn't want these folks to think, "What's wrong with that silly white boy?"

With all the moanin' and noise coming from the shaded side of the trailer we didn't need any singin'. We got our bologna sandwiches and orange crush down at lunch, and then the howlin' started. Finally, the "Holy Spirit" came into the area and we heard several of the kinfolk saying, "Praise the Lord." Yes siree, this is what you'd call womb-to-tomb followers and God had brought a new child into the world. There was no hatred or revenge to be seen in this field nor did skin pigmentation matter. But then it was right back to the cotton field, draggin' that sack between the rows. Finally, it was quittin' time. Bring that sack in and hook it on the spring scale hangin' from the wagon and see what you're worth for the day.

At the time $4.00 was the goin' rate for pickin' a hundred pounds of cotton. I picked 90 lbs. that day and would get $3.75. This would get me into two movies with popcorn and soda to boot. Hallelujah.

Both Eric and I learned not a few but many valuable lessons when we worked in the field. First of all, stay the hell out of the way of big ass machinery. Second, be on time for dinner (lunch) because if Eric beat me to it he would get the good stuff and I'd get the scraps. And most important, race, color, creed, what food someone ate—just don't make fun of their way. If you are not humble you will be humbled if you are to fit into any society.

Hell, in my hay day I got lucky by being at the right place at the right time. Most of these groups of very down-to-earth folks worked hard. Whether they were white, black or Hispanic, I had some real respect for their work ethic. There were always a few slackers. Just like sports, slackers didn't hang around long once they started a job. Being around all this diversity of life, I felt, gave me an edge. When you feel like a part of a group of people, they can broaden your mind. Go ahead— step into their shoes. It's all right to see the world from someone else's way of thinking. You will definitely take away something that will make you grow as a person. So ENGAGE!

Field of Fluff

Gideon High School

Mr. Fenton

One thing about your high school days is that certain subjects just stick out—teachers as well. At Gideon High School, we were blessed with teachers that were well-educated; most had a master's degree and had attained tenure. Mr. Huckaby headed up the math department at GHS and eventually would get his doctorate in mathematics—he was there forever. My mom and dad had him, and my brother and I had him as well. Out of Southern respect, most called him "Mr. Huckaby," but the whiz-bangs at math could get away with calling him "Huck." I didn't fall under that category. Our English department was led by brothers Joyce, James, and John King. My Mom would call them "We three Kings." I would call them, "We three Kings that will chop your fingers off for not pulling a sentence together in the correct manner."

Back in the sixties, no one knew about ADD (attention deficit disorder). I didn't find out that I had this condition until I was 46. No wonder I drove folks nuts. It was difficult for me to take a test, focus, or do homework. Life was boring. Unless I liked the subject, it was pure hell. More than likely, everybody thought of Mark Littell as first, a good athlete, second, a nice guy (for the most part), and third, that kid who had trouble doing schoolwork. I was your B-C student with an occasional A. I had tutors and went in for early work, but what I really needed was some *real* meds—off-the-chart drugs that would slow both me *and* that brain down.

The medical world would not find out for another 15 years how to start treating this disorder, so it was tough going for a while. Fortunately, I liked science and history and did all right in those two subjects. My recall was decent in the matter of science; reading was boring, but was interesting when merged into history… so it sometimes held my attention. All classrooms in the old building had ceiling fans, and they always seemed to come into play. They seemed to be part of the inner-self and psyche of this glorious malfunction: everybody else was watching the board while I was counting the turns on the fan.

In the Bootheel it was still steamy hot in the end of August when school would start up. It was in the 90-degree range, with an 85% humidity factor. Everybody would put on their bravado—for me it was new tuff-nut jeans and a collared shirt. I was wearing a paisley shirt as this was the new flair—the Beatles wore paisley, so I would too. Saddlelock shoes were right up town as well, the brown-white-brown mix being quite dazzling for the Southern gent. I slipped in a white belt even though I wasn't Baptist. Yes, I was panache…the feather was sharp. A lot of us looked the part but still couldn't deliver. The ole peer-pressure obstacle had not changed, and the hormones were flying but had no direction. Our goal was to stay cool—the Old Spice deodorant didn't work as well back then, but the high ceilings and ceiling fans helped.

There were less than 200 students at Gideon High, so everyone knew each other's business or could figure it out. I was a sophomore in 1969, and during the summer we had heard that we were getting a new history teacher. Our outgoing history teacher, Orville Deweese, would now land as our new principal. A lot of our teachers went to Ole Miss so we knew they were well educated, and basically a bunch of Rebel rousers. Mr. Deweese was one of those that fell under another category, as he was a Mississippi State bulldog that could bark, but thankfully not bite. We called him "chrome dome" on the sly, because of his bald head.

But I found out sooner rather than later that this new teacher, Mr. Fenton, was coming in to make his mark because my dad was on the school board. He told me and Eric that Mr. Fenton was coming in all the way from Massachusetts, and that this was going to be his first position in a public-school system. *A Northerner from New England with his first teaching position…a Yankee that just crossed the Mason-Dixon Line…this should go over well.*

The American History class was made up of sophomores, juniors, and a few dumbass seniors who didn't figure it out on the first go around. We had a total of 25 or so pimpled-up kids that were eager to get through the first day jitters.

I gotta tell you, on that first day Mr. Fenton looked like a duck out of water. He really didn't announce himself just yet, but it was pretty damn quiet in the classroom…we had to get a feel for this dude. His personal dress code for the first day was good-looking shoes, nice slacks, a blue long-sleeve shirt with a tie and a tie-bar, with his blazer draped over the back of a chair. Let me tell you, he was sweating bullets. But he still hadn't said a word. I'll bet that Mr. Fenton was the first teacher at GHS that was that decked out in the last ten years.

Mr. Fenton started writing on the blackboard with his back to us. We found out later that he had done his homework and had gone to Ms. King who pulled the yearbook together. Well, Mr. Fenton was now putting names to faces. *Getting a head start on Southern folk… Yankee spy.*

Gideon, Missouri was blessed with good-looking chicks and Jamie Lawrence was one of 'em. She was also the head majorette in the GHS band. Our band was no slouch—we would carry 90 in parades and in "battle of the bands" competitions. Jamie chose to sit in the front row so she stood out more, but she wasn't classified one of those "du-da" girls either—you know, "my Daddy do dis and my daddy do dat and I drive da 'vette." Danny Cleaves was a junior and a damn good basketball player, a 6'2" athlete who was mischievous at times. He sat right behind Jamie. I sat caddy corner to both on the first day of class.

Now everybody knew that Chuck Holomon and Jamie Lawrence were tight. As a matter of fact, two years later they were married. Danny Cleaves, however, must have been bored so he started popping her bra, and of course Jamie lets out a subtle *"oough"* sigh. A real slight snicker came from the students who saw what had happened, me included.

Mr. Fenton turned around and said, "Miss Lawrence, do you have a problem? Is everything all right?"

Wow, he dropped a "Miss Lawrence"—that was some high-cotton shit.

"No, just fine, sir."

Mr. Fenton turned around and went back to the blackboard. And Danny, he went back to the well one more time. The pop was a little louder this time, and so was Jamie as she let out the same *"oough."*

Not the same with Mr. Fenton, though. He walked away from the blackboard, passed Jamie's desk, and stood over Danny. "Mr. Cleaves, don't do that again, this behavior is not acceptable."

Then Fenton slapped him!

Are you shittin' me?

The whole class was stunned. After a second of silence, Danny stood up and smoked him.

A few of us grabbed Danny and tried to bring some calmness to the situation. Mr. Fenton recovered and took charge saying, "Mr. Cleaves, we're going to the office now." He took Danny by the arm. "Now!"

You can only imagine the chatter in the classroom for the next three minutes as Mr. Fenton escorted Danny down the stairs to the office. When he came back through the door, you could truly hear a needle drop.

"My name is James F. Fenton Jr., and we will be covering American history, with emphasis on the Constitution and the American Revolution."

Mr. Fenton did stand his ground, even though we thought the South was going to rise again at any moment. *Scallywag, funny accent, and Danny got a ten-day suspension.*

All went well for the next few weeks, and then we got out of school for two weeks of "cotton vacation." This cotton vacation was a must for the farmers because every hand was needed to get the cotton out of the field. There was a lot of cotton and you sure didn't need a setback like rain. It was a busy time of year for kids who grew up on a farm or in town; there was money to be made for everyone. And Eric and I would get our turn to show Mr. Fenton the ropes of pickin' cotton.

Since opening day at school, most of the kids were still cool to Mr. Fenton. Danny came back to class, sat in the back, and, yes, the Constitution survived. Since my Dad was on the school board, he was always bumping into teachers at the early season football games, the grocery store, church, the drug store—you couldn't avoid anybody in this metropolis. Dad told us that Mr.

Fenton would be coming out for dinner, and that, "You boys could show him how a cotton picker works."

We were out in the field across from the house and had the International Harvester cotton picker just a'hummin'…it was, of course, red. Eric was driving and I was sitting above him where the cage parted. I looked up and saw James F. Fenton Jr. traipsing across the field towards us. He was going across the rows knocking stalks down—*dumbass. Walk in line with the rows…typical Yankee shit.* He made it over to where we were coming through the rows with the two-row cotton picker. Eric shut it down and we both said, "Hi, Mr. Fenton."

"Hey, guys, your Dad said you would show me how you pick cotton."

"Yes, sir, we sure will, Mr. Fenton."

Then these bad spirits started floating in my head. I paused and said, "Yeah, we'll let you see all the cotton you want. We'll put you up in the cage where you can see and feel the cotton—it just keeps spittin' out."

Eric gave me that over-the-shoulder beeline stare but didn't say anything.

We told Mr. Fenton that we were going to start up the picker and then we'd open up the cage. The hydraulics had to come up to speed to lift the cage. Before we cranked up the picker, Eric and I showed Mr.

Fenton where to step so he could get up and into the cage. We turned the engine over and motioned for the Yank—I mean, Mr. Fenton—to start his ascent. Where to step was important, as he now made his way toward the top where the cage was setting.

Eric pulled the lever to open the hatch. I was yelling for Mr. Fenton to just jump in—the cage was half-full so he would like landing in all of that white fluffy stuff. Of course, the picker was loud and he couldn't hear me and I couldn't hear him, so I waved "goodbye" as the hydraulics lowered the lid of the cage. It closed and I locked it down. Eric yelled at me over the noise of the picker and said, "You'll kill him! He's going to be packed in real hard once we start running up the rows!"

I yelled back, "He'll find his way to the metal webbing that lines the cage. Yankee ingenuity should kick in…let's go!"

We finished to the end row and made a swing back through the field. When we stopped, Eric yelled, "Where's he at?"

I looked around the side and saw two hands and a mouth pressed up against the webbing. Mr. Fenton was packed in like a sardine in mustard sauce. I motioned to Eric while pointing to my mouth (open like a fish), and gave Eric the "thumbs up"—Mr. Fenton figured it out. The spindles were turning and grabbing the cotton and were then sucked up into the cage. Under and around the cage the engine sounded like a scrambler at a carnival. But from where we were setting it was a lot quieter. James F. on the other hand couldn't hear a damn word we were saying. Eric yelled, "How you going to get him out?"

"Just dump him over and into the cotton trailer—it's half full."

Eric yelled back, "You'll smother him!"

"I'll jump in and dig him out."

Eric shook his head like, "This ain't goina work."

I gave the thumbs up as he pulled up to the cotton trailer, which was about eight feet from the ground to the top rim. We pulled to the side of the trailer and disengaged the spindles. I unlocked the cage, and Eric pulled the lever for the hydraulics to kick in and lift it up. It was a pretty sight. Out came cotton, then James F. Fenton Jr., then more cotton. I was on the top rim of the cotton trailer, on point just like a bird dog getting ready to flush a covey of quail. When that last bit of cotton emptied into the trailer, I jumped in to dig his Yankee ass out.

I found him pretty quickly—he was spittin' out lint and stumbling around like a baby duck that just hatched. Eric shut off the picker and I got Mr. Fenton to the side of the trailer. At this point, he was out of breath and awkward with his speech as he slowly said, "You could have killed me."

"Naw, you were OK—but you did see a hell of a lot of cotton, didn't ya?"

He made it down out of the trailer and we walked toward the house, up the end rows. He was starting to lighten up, but he had cotton all over him. Eric parked the picker and caught up, and all three of us walked into the house where Mom and Dad were waiting. Dad immediately saw the results. Mr. Fenton said that it was quite a ride. And, of course, Dad turned to use and said, "Boys, come outside for a minute."

We knew we're goina be on Dad's shit list. He said without any hesitation, "You put him in the cage, right?"

We didn't hesitate either. "Yes, sir."

He set our ass right in about two minutes. We walked back in like nothing happened, sat down at the dinner table, and said grace. Mom's food was, as usual, out of sight. Eric and I made eye contact as we looked at Mr. Fenton talking with Mom and Dad. We grinned and chuckled under our breath at all the lint that was still floating around his hair and shirt.

Mr. Fenton was still there for my senior year, and I'll say this: he held his own and didn't back down. Yes sir, he sure came out of left field, but the American history was never dull.

Couldn't Hold Out

My blood was runnin' thick with baseball and I just couldn't hold out any longer. I know I said there wouldn't be any baseball stories in this book, but I had to sneak one in.

Brother Eric caught me and we could scare the shit outta some guys coming to the plate. The batter comin' to the plate damn well knew that if he was hit by one of my fastballs, he'd have a bullseye of a bruise the next day. And yes, it do smart when hit. Players were not the only ones exposed in open season—a bad umpire who didn't see things the right way was also ripe enough for pickin'.

When I threw well it was fun times. Eric and I had some mental telepathy goin' on when things on the field started to sour. We felt like we could fix just about anything.

When we played high school ball or American Legion baseball, an umpire would sometimes get stubborn and downright hard-headed. The umps back then had a mask with straps but no helmet, some shin guards made outta high-end plastic, and to top it off they had this black, blow-up rubber duck of a chest protector for the mid-section. There were no Nutty Buddy's around at the time, so they were squeezed and had good reason to be semi-pissed off.

During one of our high school games my senior year, we were playing on our home field, the same ball park where I took my first at bat at age six. The field was the same, the crowd was about the same, the ball players in the other dugout were, well, the same. Baseball in Gideon was one of the things you could always count on.

In the third inning I remember good ole Gideon High school takin' a 3–0 lead and it seemed like all of a sudden this umpire wanted to even the score back up. What I mean is the strike zone just seemed to narrow and get smaller. I really never griped at umps, but would wake one up when the plate got smaller than seventeen inches.

Halfway through the game, Eric had had enough, so he gave me the sign to, "Wake up the ump!" The sign was simple: Eric would point to his mask, then with his glove hand and throwing hand, start motioning like he was backin' up a semi-truck. Now it was my turn. Wind up and let 'er fly.

Well, on this particular day, the ball went between Brother Eric's mask and mitt and landed smack dab in the center of the umpire's mask. Well, my goodness, this ball knocked him back a couple of feet, but somehow he was still standing. He took off the mask and bent over at the waist, just shakin' his head like a wet dog.

Eric took off his mask too, then propped his catching mitt up on the side of his hip as he bent one knee and settled in on the commander's stance. I know what Eric was thinkin' while watching this guy recover: "Bet you didn't have your bowl of 'Wheaties' this mornin'."

For about twenty seconds he carried on in front of both teams. Yep, it was a sight to see!

Well, Eric was still holdin' his ground, when all of a sudden this umpire decided to get up close and personal. Eric hardly ever gets riled up and he kept his cool as Mr. Umpire came up right in his face and said, "You do that shit again and I'll kick your ass out."

Eric's response was, "You're not goina kick me out … I'm the only guy that can catch him."

He turned around and squatted, giving me a fastball sign, as the umpire sounded off. And it's a strike. Shutout, GAME OVER.

Gideon Baseball Team (circa) 1905

Coming Attraction

Yes siree folks, farm life and a few baseball games will definitely keep rednecks happy. Hang on because I got another one comin' and I'm goina be going through coaching days. I start down-under in Australia where there's all kinds of curious things goin' on. Hang loose.

Country Boy:
What's Up Ramrod?

Couldn't Hold Out

About the Author

Mark Littell is a former professional baseball player who pitched in the Major Leagues for the Kansas City Royals and St. Louis Cardinals. He was born in Cape Girardeau but grew up in the lower Bootheel of Missouri where he started honing his baseball skills at an early age. Mark was signed by the Royals in 1971 and was on a personal fast track when he made his debut on June 14th, 1973 in Baltimore. In 1978 he was traded to the Cardinals where he finished out his career in 1982.

After leaving the MLB and down the line, Mark served as coach in-residence for Australia's Bicentennial in 1988. He would spend three more seasons "down under." He then became a minor league pitching coach with San Diego, Milwaukee, Kansas City, and the Dodgers covering a span of 18 years. He played winter ball in Puerto Rico, coached and played in Dominican Republic, and was the speaker on the pitching phase for the Panamanian Baseball Federation.

Mark is also the inventor of the Nutty Buddy, a protective cup that won top honors from the Industrial Design Society of America. Mark remains active in the game with several club and two collegiate teams in Phoenix. He is a motivational speaker and is constantly working with players to move forward to that next level. In 2016, Mark was inducted into the Missouri Sports Hall of Fame. He currently lives in Phoenix, Arizona with his wife Sanna.

If you enjoyed this book

please share your opinion

with others on Amazon.com.

We would love to hear

what you have to say

and greatly appreciate

your support.

86333403R00115

Made in the USA
Columbia, SC
12 January 2018